THE **ESSENTIAL** BUYER'S GUIDE

BMW

X5

First generation (E53) models – 1999 to 2006

Your marque expert:
Tim Saunders

VELOCE PUBLISHING
THE PUBLISHER OF FINE AUTOMOTIVE BOOKS

Essential Buyer's Guide Series
Alfa GT (Booker)
Alfa Romeo Spider Giulia (Booker & Talbott)
Austin Seven (Barker)
Big Healeys (Trummel)
BMW E21 3 Series (1975-1983) (Reverente, Cook)
BMW GS (Henshaw)
BSA Bantam (Henshaw)
BSA 500 & 650 Twins (Henshaw)
Citroën 2CV (Paxton)
Citroën ID & DS (Heilig)
Cobra Replicas (Ayre)
Corvette C2 Sting Ray 1963-1967 (Falconer)
Ducati Bevel Twins (Falloon)
Fiat 500 & 600 (Bobbitt)
Ford Capri (Paxton)
Harley-Davidson Big Twins (Henshaw)
Hinckley Triumph triples & fours 750, 900, 955, 1000, 1050, 1200 – 1991-2009 (Henshaw)
Honda CBR600 Hurricane (Henshaw)
Honda CBR FireBlade (Henshaw)
Honda SOHC fours 1969-1984 (Henshaw)
Jaguar E-type 3.8 & 4.2-litre (Crespin)
Jaguar E-type V12 5.3-litre (Crespin)
Jaguar XJ 1995-2003 (Crespin)
Jaguar XK8 & XKR (1996-2005) (Thorley)
Jaguar/Daimler XJ6, XJ12 & Sovereign (Crespin)
Jaguar/Daimler XJ40 (Crespin)
Jaguar Mark 1 & 2 (All models including Daimler 2.5-litre V8) 1955 to 1969 (Thorley)
Jaguar S-type – 1999 to 2007 (Thorley)
Jaguar X-type – 2001 to 2009 (Thorley)
Jaguar XJ-S (Crespin)
Jaguar XJ6, XJ8 & XJR (Thorley)
Jaugar XK 120, 140 & 150 (Thorley)
Land Rover Series I, II & IIA (Thurman)
Mazda MX-5 Miata (Mk1 1989-97 & Mk2 98-2001) (Crook)
Mercedes-Benz 280SL-560DSL Roadsters (Bass)
Mercedes-Benz 'Pagoda' 230SL, 250SL & 280SL
Roadsters & Coupés (Bass)
MGA 1955-1962 (Sear, Crosier)
MGB & MGB GT (Williams)
MG Midget & A-H Sprite (Horler)
MG TD, TF & TF1500 (Jones)
Mini (Paxton)
Morris Minor & 1000 (Newell)
New Mini (Collins)
Norton Commando (Henshaw)
Peugeot 205 GTI (Blackburn)
Porsche 911 (930) Turbo series (Streather)
Porsche 911 (964) (Streather)
Porsche 911 (993) (Streather)
Porsche 911 (996) (Streather)
Porsche 911 Carrera 3.2 series 1984 to 1989 (Streather)
Porsche 911SC – Coupé, Targa, Cabriolet & RS Model years 1978-1983 (Streather)
Porsche 924 – All models 1976 to 1988 (Hodgkins)
Porsche 928 (Hemmings)
Porsche 986 Boxster series (Streather)
Porsche 987 Boxster and Cayman series (Streather)
Rolls-Royce Silver Shadow & Bentley T-Series (Bobbitt)
Subaru Impreza (Hobbs)
Triumph Bonneville (Henshaw)
Triumph Spitfire & GT6 (Baugues)
Triumph Stag (Mort & Fox)
Triumph TR7 & TR8 (Williams)
Vespa Scooters – Classic 2-stroke models 1960-2008 (Paxton)
VW Beetle (Cservenka & Copping)
VW Bus (Cservenka & Copping)
VW Golf GTI (Cservenka & Copping)

www.veloce.co.uk

First published in September 2013 by Veloce Publishing Limited, Veloce House, Parkway Farm Business Park, Middle Farm Way, Poundbury, Dorchester, Dorset, DT1 3AR, England.
Fax 01305 250479/e-mail info@veloce.co.uk/web www.veloce.co.uk or www.velocebooks.com.

ISBN: 978-1-845845-33-9 UPC: 6-36847-04533-3

Introduction
– the purpose of this book

Over a seven year period the BMW X5 E53, which was in production from 1999 to 2006 (when the E70 was launched), established an unrivalled reputation as the ultimate luxury 4x4, and a loyal celebrity following.

On the outside, the X5 is striking, and arguably more up-to-date and appealing than any Range Rover or Mercedes off-roader of the same age. Even though the first models are now well over a decade old they still look fresh. The Bavarian beast is a successful marriage of lines and curves – its fairly boxy and angular rear stands in contrast to its comparatively rounded bonnet, home to the famous BMW logo and double-kidney grille. Overall, the design is very pleasing to the eye. Add to the mix typically strong German build quality, together with a luxurious interior and a decent range of engines ...

The X5 has been particularly popular amongst sports personalities. Seven times world snooker champion Stephen Hendry owned a 2005 4.8-litre V8 M-Spec X5 finished in burgundy. It was put up for sale three years later and advertised in *Auto Trader* with 52,000 miles on the clock and a £16,995 price tag.

In 2004, midfielder Steven Gerrard, who went on to become England and Liverpool captain, purchased a grey 4.8-litre V8 X5, setting him back over £66,000. In 2008, with 34,000 miles, it was advertised in *Auto Trader* for £24,950. Rio Ferdinand, the Manchester United central defender owned a black X5 3-litre diesel Sport in 2003, fitted with two televisions in the rear. In 2007, this model with just 26,000 miles on the clock was being sold in *Auto Trader* for £25,995.

Ex-England and Newcastle United manager Sir Bobby Robson bought a silver 3-litre X5 in 2002, quite possibly on the recommendation of Wes Brown, the England international footballer. Brown purchased a black X5 4.4-litre V8 in 2001, complete with 22-inch alloy wheels and £4500 worth of audio equipment, including subwoofer speakers and a 9-inch pull down TV-DVD. In 2008 this clearly well used example was for sale in *Auto Trader* for just £12,494. Wes Brown set the ball rolling for the BMW X5 to gain notoriety among Britain's footballing elite.

In 2002, British boxing legend Frank Bruno, who won the WBC (World Boxing Council) boxing championship, purchased an eye-catching metallic blue BMW X5 4.4-litre V8 incorporating TV screens and a Sony PlayStation. In 2007, having covered 60,000 miles, it was being sold in *Auto Trader* for £21,495.

Other celebrities to have owned an X5 E53 include *Holby City* star Patsy Kensit, who bought a black X5 3-litre injection Sport, for more than £37,000. In 2008 this was advertised for sale in *Auto Trader* for £14,995, having covered 54,000 miles.

Former Atomic Kitten and reality TV star Kerry Katona purchased a good used silver BMW X5 E53 in 2010, and was pictured with it in the *Daily Mail* newspaper.

Popular also among business people and property developers it typically doesn't venture off road. It has more than ample legroom for tall drivers and passengers, and is a versatile vehicle for those with families.

The BMW X5 was named the most stolen vehicle of 2010, according to vehicle recovery expert Tracker.

It's an SAV (Sports Activity Vehicle), a crossover that uses a monocoque (single shell) construction, like most cars today, and, importantly, it drives like a sports car.

These two key characteristics set it apart from SUVs (Sport Utility Vehicles) such as the Land Rover Range Rover.

This 4x4 is not as capable as the long-established Range Rover, with which it shares some technology, but, perhaps because of its appeal to affluent urban types looking to make a statement, that hasn't hindered its success.

Thanks

My personal thanks go to all those who have contributed to this publication, in particular Hampshire entrepreneur Wally Pickett, for the use of his cherished BMW X5 E53. My wife Caroline has provided invaluable assistance in taking photographs, proofreading and organising me! Sharon Ellis, Finance Director at Bartley BMW in Totton, Southampton provided expert advice, comments and images. FAB Recycling Ltd in Gloucestershire supplied images of distressed BMW X5 E53s, while Martin Harrison, Media Relations Officer at BMW UK has shown support and encouragement for this project, not least in supplying photographs and information. Parkers, the long established and renowned car expert, has provided useful and informative comments.

The Intimidator: BMW X5 E53.

Contents

THE ESSENTIAL BUYER'S GUIDE™ CURRENCY

At the time of publication a BG unit of currency "●" equals approximately £1.00/ US$1.53/Euro 1.17. Please adjust to suit current exchange rates using Sterling as the base currency.

1 Is it the right car for you?
– marriage guidance

Tall and short drivers
The BMW X5 E53 has plenty of leg and headroom for tall drivers and passengers. And so it's no surprise that tall celebrities (of six feet and above), including footballers Steven Gerrard and Rio Ferdinand, snooker ace Stephen Hendry, and former boxer and pantomime star Frank Bruno, have all owned one. But it will also accommodate shorter drivers, such as actress Patsy Kensit – a petite five feet and four inches tall. This demonstrates the user-friendliness of this prestigious vehicle.

Weight of controls
Light and easy to handle, all have power assisted steering and brakes.

Will it fit in the garage?
Length: 183.7in, 466.598cm or 4666mm (six inches shorter than a BMW 5-series)
Width: 73.7in, 187.198cm or 1871.98mm (wider than a BMW 7-series)
Height: 67.2in, 170.688cm or 1706.88mm although some models vary, as explained later.

Emissions summary
Parkers, the car expert, sounds a note of caution: "The X5 performs badly on the eco front. With an average of 287g/km CO_2 across the line-up, its emissions are high for a large 4x4. However, it's worth noting that the line-up has a high number of diesel models, bringing the average down and giving buyers more choices of low-emission versions. Diesels typically produce less CO_2 than petrol engines with similar power outputs. The range is quite thirsty, averaging 25mpg."

It adds: "All models have electronic self-levelling suspension, alloy wheels, park distance control, cruise control, remote central locking, electric heated door mirrors. Sport models add 19-in alloy wheels, uprated suspension, while the 4.6iS has 20-inch alloys, flared wheelarches, twin exhaust pipes and rear head and side airbags. Options include adaptive headlights that swivel on corners."

Luxurious surroundings with plenty of room make the X5 ideal for tall drivers and passengers.

Interior space
"This luxury 4x4 has enough room to transport five adults in absolute comfort," says Parkers. "There is plenty of legroom in the front and back. Headroom all round is a good size, and there is plenty of elbow room, with most front and rear seat occupants finding these vehicles very comfortable."

Luggage capacity
"The BMW X5 has a massive boot, making it a very versatile vehicle," says Parkers. "The mammoth boot makes light work of virtually any load, meaning that it is a vehicle of choice for many developers. It effectively doubles up as a family runabout coping well with all the associated paraphernalia of children. There is plenty of space to stretch out."

The complete tailgate open: boot space is excellent.

The bottom half of the split tailgate up.

Usability
A practical car in all conditions.

Parts availability
Nearly everything is still available through the many specialists around. Good tested used parts can also be acquired.

Parts cost
Still a modern car, many items are only available from BMW, and, as a consequence, are not cheap. Lazy garages have a tendency to replace rather than attempt to repair parts, which is inevitably more costly.

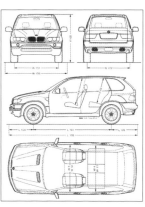

BMW X5 E53 height and width.

Overall, BMW X5 parts prices are expensive.

A solution to the problem is to find a reputable independent dealership, such as Bartley Independent BMW Specialists in Totton, Hampshire, which (so Finance Director Sharon Ellis claims) can be as much as 50 per cent cheaper than a BMW dealer.

Investment potential
When the first examples of the BMW X5 hit 20 years old, they could be considered classics, certainly by insurance companies, and so prices of the very finest versions could rise while insurance premiums should decline. However, BMW has sold over one million X5s (E53 and E70), and this, due to the nature of supply and demand as well as high oil prices, could severely limit the long-term investment potential.

Alternatives
Audi Q7, Infiniti FX, Jeep Grand Cherokee, Mercedes M-Class, Porsche Cayenne, Range Rover, Toyota Landcruiser, Volkswagen Touareg, Volvo XC60 and Volvo XC90.

Bavarian beast: BMW X5 E53.

2 Cost considerations
– affordable, or a money pit?

Purchase price

Buy the best X5 E53 that funds allow. A more expensive model in good condition is a far better proposition than a cheaper one requiring a good deal of work. Service history is vital, and it doesn't matter whether it has been maintained by a franchised dealer or an independent. While an up-to-date service book is a good sign, look for proof that the work has actually been carried out. Overall, owners of brand new X5 E53s lost considerable amounts of money as soon as they drove off the forecourt. Now that prices have reached rock bottom, some examples can cost the same as a used Ford Fiesta. Therefore, the X5 E53 now makes a much better long-term proposition, and is positively good value for money.

Servicing

Typical intervals are:

Regular service: 15,000 miles (indicator appears on the dash – the work carried out on each service is listed in the owner's handbook, depends on model and engine)

Renew sparkplugs: 35,000 miles (although it's possible to fit long-life sparkplugs that last for 100,000 miles)

Renew air filter: 30,000 miles

Major service: 60,000 miles

Parts prices (approximate) at an independent BMW specialist. Add 50 per cent for a franchised dealer:

Standard scope ●20
Vehicle check ●108
Intake silencer ●110
Fuel filter ●114
Micro filter ●111
Brake fluid ●61
Oil service ●205
Oil service ●250 (includes micro filter)
Third oil service ●550 (includes a fuel filter and air filter)
Rear brake pads ●234
Front brake pads ●281
Brake discs vented (front) ●150
Brake pads vented (rear) ●150

Brake discs (rear) ●150
Water pump ●700
Thermostat with map sensor ●49
Front shock absorbers ●200
Rear shock absorbers ●200
Wheel bearings ●42
Left and right wishbone bushes ●180
Xenon headlamp unit ●159

Used parts

There's a plentiful supply, but make sure that they are tested before purchase. Many refurbished parts are now also available.

So many X5 E53s were produced that there's a good supply of used, parts to keep costs down.

Buy the best you can afford; it's cheaper in the long run.

3 Living with a BMW X5

– will you get along together?

Good points

One of the top status symbols on the road at an affordable price
Commanding view of the road
Sophisticated and refined
Excellent ride and handling
Spacious with comfortable seats
Attractive and well designed; it's still fresh
Strong performance
Generally good build quality
Robust engines

Bad points

Thirsty
Environmentally unfriendly
Expensive servicing and parts
High insurance and road tax
Interior trim and switches are prone to breakage

Summary

This well-styled king of the road is capable, versatile, and a great drive. A used example in good condition represents a good long-term investment. Buy the best possible to guard against unnecessary expense.

Great looks and practicality – a capable all-round vehicle.

4 Relative values

Models

The model range is quite simple: one body style with seven engines.

3-litre injection six-cylinder petrol (2001 to 2006)
Engine: M54B30
Power: 228bhp
0-60mph: 8.8sec
Top speed. 120mph

3-litre diesel (2001 to 2003)
Engine: M57D30
Power: 182bhp
0-60mph: 10.1sec
Top speed: 130mph

Early X5 E53 3-litre diesel with V-spoke style 63 alloy wheels.

3-litre in-line six-cylinder (2004 to 2006)
Engine: M57TUD30
Power: 215bhp
0-60mph: 8.8sec
Top speed: 146mph

4.4-litre V8 petrol (2000 to 2003)
Engine: M62TUB44
Power: 282bhp
0-60mph: 7.6sec
Top speed: 140mph

4.4-litre V8 petrol (2004 to 2006)
Engine: N62B44
Power: 316bhp
0-60mph: 7sec
Top speed: 150mph

Early X5 E53 4.4i petrol with star-spoke style 132 alloy wheels.

4.6-litre is V8 petrol (2001 to 2003)
Engine: M62B46
Power: 335bhp
0-60mph: 7sec
Top speed: 151mph

4.8-litre is V8 petrol (2004 to 2006)
Engine: N62B48
Power: 350bhp
0-60mph: 6.1sec
Top speed: 153mph

Robust and practical interior is a little basic on the entry level 3-litre diesel.

The best all-rounder is the three-litre diesel model because it boasts strong performance and the best mpg readings of the range, while also producing lower CO2 emissions.

Values

When the BMW X5 E53 was in production, between 1999 and 2006, a brand new one would have set you back anywhere from £33,955 to £65,082.

This type of vehicle, along with other Chelsea tractors, is unpopular among environmentalists, namely because of its notable fuel inefficiency and high emissions. But it is not a patch on the notorious Hummer.

As a result, the X5 E53 has experienced hefty depreciation, which at best, for a pristine example, is 50 per cent of the original OTR (on the road) price, and at worst, just three per cent. When purchased new this was one of the best ways of burning money.

However, such a cataclysmic drop in value makes the X5 E53 a splendid used purchase because prices cannot drop much further.

L-R: BMW X5 E70 (second generation launched in 2006), and X5 E53 (first generation). The E53 is boxier, and perhaps more purposeful-looking.

5 Before you view
– be well informed

To avoid a wasted journey, and the disappointment of finding that the car does not match your expectations, it will help if you're very clear about the questions you want to ask before you pick up the telephone. Some of these points might appear basic, but when you're excited about the prospect of buying your dream classic, it's amazing how some of the most obvious things slip the mind ... Also check the current values of your favoured model in classic car magazines; these give both a price guide and auction results.

Condition is everything but an owner's view is often biased.

Where is the car?
Is it going to be worth travelling to the next county/state, or even across a border? A locally advertised car, although it may not sound very interesting, can add to your knowledge for very little effort, so make a visit – it might even be in better condition than expected.

Dealer or private sale?
Establish early on if the car is being sold by its owner or by a trader. A private owner should have all the history, so don't be afraid to ask detailed questions. A dealer may have more limited knowledge of a vehicle's history, but should have some documentation. A dealer may offer a warranty/guarantee (ask for a printed copy) and finance.

Cost of collection and delivery
A dealer may well be used to quoting for delivery by car transporter. A private owner may agree to meet you halfway, but only agree to this after you've seen the vehicle at the vendor's address to validate the documents. Conversely, you could meet halfway and agree the sale, but insist on meeting at the vendor's address for the handover.

View – when and where
It is always preferable to view at the vendor's home or business premises. In the case of a private sale, the vehicle's documentation should tally with the vendor's name and address. Arrange to view only in daylight and avoid a wet day. Most vehicles look better in poor light or when wet.

Reason for sale?
Do make it one of the first questions. Why is the vehicle being sold and how long has it been with the current owner? How many previous owners?

Left-hand drive to right-hand drive/specials and convertibles

If a steering conversion has been done it can only reduce the value, and it may well be that other aspects of the vehicle still reflect the specification for a foreign market.

Condition (body/chassis/interior/mechanicals)?

Ask for an honest appraisal of the vehicle's condition. Ask specifically about some of the check items described in chapter 7.

All original specification?

An original equipment vehicle is invariably of higher value than a customised version.

Matching data/legal ownership

Do VIN/chassis/engine numbers and license plate match the official registration document? Is the owner's name and address recorded in the official registration documents?

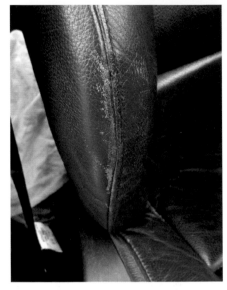

A worn driver's seat is a sign of high mileage.

For those countries requiring an annual test of roadworthiness, does the vehicle have a document showing it complies (an MoT certificate in the UK, which can be verified on 0845 600 5977)?

If a smog/emissions certificate is mandatory, does the car have one?

If required, does the vehicle carry a current road fund license/license plate tag?

Does the vendor own the vehicle outright? Money might be owed to a finance company or bank: the vehicle could even be stolen. Several organisations will supply the data on

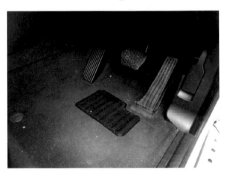

A well presented footwell can be a sign of a low mileage vehicle.

ownership, based on the vehicle's licence plate number, for a fee. Such companies can often also tell you whether the car has been 'written off' by an insurance company. In the UK these organisations can supply vehicle data:

HPI – 01722 422 422
AA – 0870 600 0836
DVLA – 0870 240 0010
RAC – 0870 533 3660

Other countries will have similar organisations.

Unleaded fuel
If necessary, has the car been modified to run on unleaded fuel?

Insurance
Check with your existing insurer before setting out – your current policy might not cover you to drive the car if you do purchase it.

How you can pay?
A cheque/check will take several days to clear, and the seller may prefer to sell to a cash buyer. However, a banker's draft (a cheque issued by a bank) is a good as cash, but safer, so contact your own bank and become familiar with the formalities necessary to obtain one.

Buying at auction?
If the intention is to buy at auction see chapter 10 for further advice.

Professional vehicle check (mechanical examination)
There are often marque/model specialists who will undertake professional examinations of a vehicle on your behalf. Owners clubs will be able to put you in touch with such specialists.

Other organisations that will carry out a general professional check (in the UK) are:

AA – 0800 085 3007 (motoring organisation with vehicle inspectors)
ABS – 0800 358 5855 (specialist vehicle inspection company)
RAC – 0870 533 3660 (motoring organisation with vehicle inspectors)

Other countries will have similar organisations.

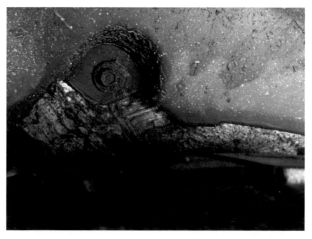

There should be no rust under the wheelarches.

6 Inspection equipment
– these items will really help

This book
Reading glasses (if you need them for close work)
Magnet (not powerful, a fridge magnet is ideal)
Torch
Probe (a small screwdriver works very well)
Overalls
Mirror on a stick
Digital camera
A friend, preferably a knowledgeable enthusiast

It's worthwhile getting the X5 on a ramp and giving it a thorough inspection.

Before you rush out of the door, gather together a few items that will help as you work your way around the vehicle. This book is designed to be your guide at every step, so take it along and use the check boxes in chapter 9 to help you assess each area of the vehicle. Don't be afraid to let the seller see you using it. Take your reading glasses if you need them to read documents and make close up inspections.

A knowledgeable enthusiast can help when checking an intended buy.

A magnet will help you check if the X5 is full of filler, or has fibreglass panels. Use the magnet to sample bodywork areas all around the car, but be careful not to damage the paintwork. Expect to find a little filler here and there, but not whole panels. There's nothing wrong with fibreglass panels, but a purist might want the car to be as original as possible.

A torch with fresh batteries will be useful for peering into the wheelarches and under the vehicle.

A small screwdriver can be used (with care) as a probe, particularly in the wheelarches and on the underside, to check an area of severe corrosion. Be careful, though – if it's really bad the screwdriver might go right through the metal!

Be prepared to get dirty. Take along a pair of overalls. Fixing a mirror at an angle on the end of a stick may seem odd, but you'll probably need it to check the condition of the underside of the vehicle. It will also help you to peer into some of the important crevices. You can also use it, together with the torch, along the underside of the sills and on the floor.

If you have the use of a digital camera, take it along so that later you can study some areas of the vehicle more closely. Take a picture of any part of the X5 that causes you concern, and seek a friend's opinion.

Ideally, have a friend or knowledgeable enthusiast accompany you: a second opinion is always valuable.

7 Fifteen minute evaluation
– walk away or stay?

Road test

My road test was conducted using a 2002-registered three-litre diesel, purchased by Wally Pickett from Shedfield in Hampshire in 2007. The 12,000-mile vehicle – complete with private number plate, X55 URF (X5 SURF) – cost £19,000. Wally sold his Mercedes ML 300 for £5000, which he put towards his new purchase.

A road test over a variety of surfaces is a must when considering an X5.

The first thing to do when evaluating an X5 is to sit in the driver's seat and check that all the controls work, including the electric windows and wing mirrors; broken or defective motors can be expensive to rectify. Turn on the ignition and the diesel engine will make a typical rattle. This will be audible from the outside but, thanks to good quality soundproofing, cannot be heard from inside. If, however, the engine rattles more than expected on start-up, and/or it is audible inside the car, this could indicate timing issues. At this point it's advisable to look in the rear view mirror (or check at the rear of the car) for blue smoke, the sign of an abused engine. New engines aren't cheap, and it's far better to pay a bit more for a well-looked-after vehicle than to buy a cheaper, poor quality example.

A clean engine is always a good sign.

The doors should shut with a satisfying clunk.

Although often criticised for the amount of black in the interior (on the dash, the doors and the seats), the interior

The driver's seat is the first area to suffer wear and tear.

Check overall condition of the interior.

is hardwearing, and the black leather seats are comfortable and supportive, ensuring that all passengers reach their destination in a relaxed state, even after long journeys.

Try all switches, including those on the driver's seat, to make sure everything is functioning correctly.

When an X5 is chipped for improved performance and fuel economy, this box of tricks is fitted. All extra equipment should be tested.

Test all gear positions.

Check the dials work. For a vehicle to be roadworthy it must be fitted with a working speedometer. Broken speedometers incur a fine and MoT failure.

"It costs me £500 a year to insure with fully comprehensive cover," says Wally (78). He adds: "It's been chipped for better fuel economy. On long journeys I now get around 34mpg, whereas before I'd get just 25mpg."

Wally takes his wife to the shops in his X5 and drives it to Lancashire and Wales to see relatives. During the week it sits on the driveway at home while he uses his pickup truck for work.

Of his X5 he says: "I have never serviced it, but it is going to need two rear tyres soon at a cost of about £230 a pair. It's got 60,000 miles on the clock now, and I've never even topped it up with oil! It's never let me down."

Wally adds: "This X5 is worth £10,000 today because it is in tiptop condition, with no rust and low mileage for its age. It's only had two owners, and it's not going up and down the motorway seven days a week. It's been well looked after, although I've never polished it and only shampoo it every few months."

All in all the BMW X5 is a versatile vehicle, which is happier on the road but will also tackle off-roading with aplomb, if required.

General condition

BMW X5 E53s are well built, and I have

Stand back from the vehicle: you should be able to spot any discolouration, indicative of damage repair.

The nose area is the most vulnerable part of the bodywork.

A white plastic filler cap should be fitted to the windscreen wash bottle. Notoriously flimsy, this can be replaced with a cheap petrol filler cap.

Condensation in the headlamp units can be a problem.

yet to see one with rust. Leather seats hide the miles better, so pay particular attention to wear, especially on the driver's seat. Check for discolouration of the paintwork; a sign of a poor re-spray.

Engine bay
Check for leaks when the engine is running. Wally says: "When I was filling up the windscreen wash bottle the flimsy white plastic filler cap broke so I've had to replace it with a petrol filler cap. The rubber cover on the engine unit blew off in the wind."

External bodywork
Look along both sides of the vehicle, as this will highlight any minor dents or car parking scrapes, all of which can be used in your price negotiations.

By doing this I could tell that the model tested had a minor accident repair (rear right) at some point, but that it had been completed to a reasonably good standard. A critical eye picked up some paint overlap between the bumper and bodywork. Clearly the bumper had been removed and not aligned as well as it could have been. Stone chips on the bonnet may indicate fast driving, and this combined with a heavily worn driver's footwell (mat, carpet, trim) are all signs of a high mileage vehicle.

Damaged alloy wheels can prove expensive to repair or replace.

The windscreen is another common stone chip area.

Plastic trim can hide rust.

Interior

Particular attention should be paid to the interior, as this can reveal a whole host of expensive problems. A bit like an old house, you'll either get a good feeling on first acquaintance or not as the case may be. Critically assess the door and roof panels. Do they look as if they've been removed and refitted? Is there any broken trim? This could mean that the electrics have been repaired. Check that all the electric windows rise and fall without making a whirring noise. Noisy and/or slow operation is a warning that the electric motor will soon fail, and it will be expensive to repair. Do the same with the electric mirrors. Do any warning lights appear when the ignition is turned? This is a sign of more expense.

Pay attention to the digital central display. "When I first bought it I was fiddling about with the central display

Check that the wing mirrors work.

Check that the centre console works, especially the television.

Check that all interior switches and buttons are present and intact.

to try and get the television to work but I didn't know what I was doing," admits Wally. "I was pressing so many different buttons. An anti-theft code had been installed and I didn't know what it was; still don't. Anyway, my fiddling resulted in the X5 refusing to start, as well as the doors and windows locking and I couldn't get out. So I phoned the AA who disconnected the battery for 10 minutes. They thought it was a flat battery but it wasn't and that was when we discovered that the security code was to blame. The AA set the unit to zero, which meant that I could drive the vehicle, but to this day the television only operates in black and white, is very fuzzy, and suffers from a lot of interference, which is really annoying. It

will cost as much as £2000 to repair," he concludes. The moral of the story is to ensure that you know the security code – make sure that you get this from the owner.

Turn your attention to the upholstery, ensuring that you give it much more than just a cursory glance. Thoroughly check each seat, especially the driver's seat, for cigarette burns, rips and tears. Is the driver's seat as firm and supportive as it should be? If it sags and looks as if it's seen better days, you know you're looking at a high mileage vehicle. You will know whether a smoker has owned the X5 because there will be nasty nicotine stains on the steering wheel, doors, switches and even windows. A good clean will put this right.

Usually the carpets will corroborate your overall opinion of the vehicle. If foot mats have been used the carpets will be in good order, and this is generally an indication of a careful owner.

Boot

More often than not an X5's boot is not as well cared for as you might hope, because its capaciousness makes for an effective load carrying workhorse. It will shift a plethora of items, from bicycles to furniture, and even office equipment. The test X5 had been used to transport heavy wood and machinery. If you're lucky, as was the case with the test model, a cover will have been placed over the boot, protecting it as much as possible.

The boot is home to the vehicle's battery – located under the spare wheel.

Facts at a glance
0-60mph	10.1sec
Top speed	124mph
Power	181bhp
Economy you'll be lucky to get 20mpg	

Watch the video at: www.testdrives.biz

8 Key points
– where to look for problems

Engines
Model line-up

Model	Model Year	Engine	Output (PS/kW)	0-60 (sec)
3.0i	2001–2006	M54B30	231 / 170	8.8
3.0d	2001–2003	M57D30	184 / 134	10.1
	2004–2006	M57TUD30	218 / 160	8.8
4.4i	2000–2003	M62TUB44	286 / 210	7.6
	2004–2006	N62B44	320 / 238	7.0
4.6is	2001–2003	M62B46	340 / 250	7.0
4.8is	2004–2006	N62B48	355 / 261	6.1

The BMW X5 E53 uses the same 4.4i 315bhp engine as the BMW 7-series saloon. In 2002 a sporty 4.6is V8 model, developed by Alpina from the 4.4-litre V8, with 20-inch alloy wheels was launched. Two years later the renowned engine specialist introduced a more aggressive 4.8is 355bhp, replacing the 4.6. This was used in the BMW E52 Z8, too.

Well maintained engines will go on and on.

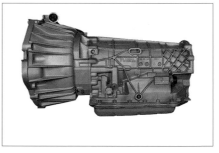

BMW X5 E53 V8 4.4L remanufactured automatic transmission. Reconditioned gearboxes don't come cheap, so beware of faults.

Gearboxes
Transmission
5-speed automatic (it's possible to buy a reconditioned one for ●850 on eBay)
5-speed manual
6-speed automatic
6-speed manual

Suspension, steering and brakes
Expensive aluminium suspension components are used on the X5 E53 with the main aim of reducing vehicle weight. With age come faults, though, so it's important to carry out as thorough an inspection as possible. This is discussed in more detail in chapter 9. Oil leaks are another all too common occurrence, and these are most likely to come from the suspension arms mounted to the subframe. Also, leaking oil

BMW X5 E53 rear axle frame suspension carrier crossmember.

Front Brembo Brake Discs – BMW X5 (E53) 4.4i V8 2000 to 2006.

can come from the power steering – heavy steering can be a give-away that there's a problem lurking.

Floorpan

The reinforced rigid floorpan is joined to the front and rear structures, and the side frames are welded to it.

A non-standard finish – gold – adorns this fine example on the Isle of Wight.

Score each section according to the values in the boxes: 4 = excellent; 3 = good; 2 = average; 1 = poor. The totting up procedure is detailed at the end of the chapter. Be realistic in your marking!

You've got this far, so now it's time to go for the step-by-step detailed inspection, before deciding whether to part with your hard-earned cash. Read, digest, check against your intended purchase, and then tick the appropriate box (excellent, good, average, poor) and total the points. Be especially vigilant with regard to the key points highlighted in chapter 8.

Former BBC *Top Gear* presenter Quentin Willson once waxed lyrical about buying vehicles that are over 10 years old because anything that is going to go wrong already has, and all major repairs have been carried out. The X5 E53 fits perfectly into this category, having been first introduced in 1999. The expert's advice, therefore, would be to go for a well-maintained early example.

Engine

3.0i M54 engine, 6-cylinder, 3.0-litre
4.4i M62 TU engine, V8, 4.4 litre
4.4i N62 engine, V8, 4.4-litre
(Valvetronic)
4.6is M62 TU engine, V8, 4.6-litre
4.8is N62 engine, V8, 4.8-litre
(Valvetronic)

Engine management systems (Motronic)
Siemens DME MS 43
Bosch DME ME 7.2
Bosch DME 9.2.1

Transmissions
Manual 5-speed S5D280Z
Manual 6-speed GS637BZ
Automatic 5-speed A5S390R
Automatic 5-speed A5S440Z
Automatic 6-speed GA6HP26Z

The sign of a well-maintained vehicle is a clean engine bay.

Generally speaking, all of the BMW X5 E53 engines listed above are well engineered, and easily capable of covering at least 300,000 miles (if regularly serviced and maintained). As with many modern vehicles, the engine is a sealed unit that only an expert mechanic can access. Is there a rubber cover over part of the engine? These can blow off in high winds as they are retained by only four plastic pins inserted into rubber grommets. Affordable replacements can be purchased from various outlets, including eBay.

It's only when you're behind the wheel that problems will truly become apparent. The X5 E53 should accelerate swiftly between gears, but if it drags its heels it could be experiencing injector issues or even failure; an expensive problem.

The drivebelts at the front of the engine must be replaced regularly, and so will need to be inspected. "No specialist tools are required, and it's a fairly straightforward job to do," says Sharon Ellis from Bartley Independent BMW Specialists in Totton, Hampshire. "But at least some mechanical knowledge would be required to do so." You should also check the timing chain tensioners; they may have started to break down, upsetting engine timing. If not addressed, these can break and cause engine failure. If you have any doubt as to whether or not they have been changed it's best to replace them; a small price to pay for peace of mind.

"There's no set schedule to change timing chain tensioners," says Sharon Ellis. "They should be changed as required, and this should be picked up during the course of normal service work."

Ever wondered what the initials BMW stand for?

The standard 3-litre diesel engine in a BMW X5 E53.

Open up: doesn't the X5 E53 look like a monster with its mouth open? Clean engine: the sign of a well looked after vehicle.

Check the condition of the drivebelts at the front of the engine.

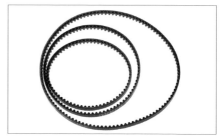

New drivebelts should be fitted regularly.

An example of a timing chain in good working order.

A BMW timing chain.

Diagnostic test  [3] [2] [1]

If you're unfamiliar with a particular vehicle, it's good practice to have a diagnostic test carried out. This will either issue a clean bill of health or highlight issues that need remedying. Part of this check is an airflow test, which registers the flow of air in metres per minute, and compares it to the factory data. Specialist garages can carry out this check, and it's only by

plugging an X5 E53 into the diagnostic machine that it's possible to know the factory standard reading, according to expert Sharon Ellis at Bartley BMW in Totton, Southampton.

Cooling system [4] [3] [2] [1]

Older vehicles can suffer from coolant leaks which, if unresolved, can cause engine overheating and subsequent damage.

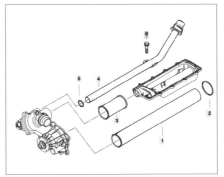

Cooling system: 1. Water pipe, feed. 2. O-ring. 3. Return pipe. 4. Return pipe, heater. 5. O-ring. 6. Hex bolt with washer.

The radiator is an essential part of the engine cooling system, and is likely to need replacing on older vehicles.

Gearbox [4] [3] [2] [1]

Particular attention must be paid to the gearbox, as this is one of the most expensive items to replace. X5 E53s are

X5s were available with automatic or manual gearboxes. Manuals are the least temperamental.

means 100,000 miles). Check for smooth gear changes, clutch wear and judder, and that no leaks are present, particularly in the transmission filter, causing the transmission oil to leak. This is a relatively small job to fix for a transmission specialist.

A problem automatic gearbox will be quite obvious because it will slip between gears. On both manual and auto gearboxes it's necessary to check whether the gears start to bounce into first when the vehicle is slowing. Does the transmission light appear on the dashboard? If so, expense is just round the corner. If the light doesn't come on, has it been disconnected? This is harder to discover without a thorough knowledge of electrics, but a good mechanic should know. It always pays to take a mechanic with you on an inspection. Interestingly, there are few reports of troublesome manual gearboxes, so perhaps it's a good idea to only consider purchasing a manual X5 ... they certainly seem to be much less of a headache.

Suspension/ steering

The suspension consists of standard self-levelling MacPherson struts at the front and air springs at the back. A good test is to push down with all your weight

renowned for their automatic gearbox troubles (although BMW denies any manufacturing fault). There are reports of automatic boxes failing on vehicles which have covered only 60,000 miles, and which have full BMW service histories. To replace an automatic box on an X5 costs between ●3000 and ●6000, depending on whether a main or an independent dealer does the work. If the X5 has an automatic gearbox it has lifetime oil (usually this

A pair of X5 E53 rear air ride suspension rings.

Front suspension can be susceptible to oil leaks.

A replacement front lower radius arm to chassis bushing set for the BMW X5 E53.

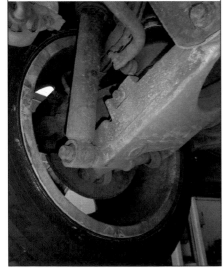

Rear suspension can be susceptible to oil leaks.

on each of the four corners of the vehicle in turn. So long as they instantly spring back up you have nothing to worry about, but squeaks, rattles, or a delay in regaining the correct stance should set off warning bells. Just to remedy worn front suspension will cost several hundred , so be thorough in your checks. Pay particular attention to the track rod ends. Is there any play on the suspension joints? It's not unusual for the CV (constant velocity) joint boot to need replacing – this allows a driveshaft to transmit power through a variable angle. They are mainly used in all-wheel drive vehicles such as the X5 E53.

Check the power steering pipe and rack for leaks. A road test will help highlight questionable suspension. A 'knocking' sound when on the move is a sure sign of broken coils or springs.

Brakes 4 3 2 1
The BMW X5 E53 weighs almost two tonnes, so its all-round discs and pads are absolutely vital. Therefore, it is extremely important to ensure that they are not excessively worn. Reaching through the alloy wheel will reveal that they have at least been securely fitted but it's harder to check the actual wear and tear. Any unexpected noises during the test drive should be investigated immediately (a screeching noise may

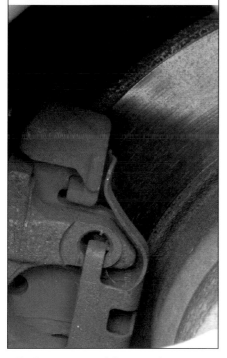

Brakes are one of the most important parts of a car, so it important to check that they are in good order.

Service (CBS) module, where a light appears on the dash when a repair needs to be carried out. This includes warnings that brake pads need to be replaced – the detail can be looked up on the iDrive computer system.

Exhaust

Check for the smell of burnt oil around the twin drainpipe exhausts. Is there a hissing sound under the valve cover? How does the valve cover gasket or exhaust manifold look? You may detect the smell of burning from oil leaks when the engine has fully warmed up (after around 50 miles). If there's an oil leak at the rear of the valve cover it can disappear as the heat from the engine makes it evaporate. This can be a common problem on vehicles with more than 100,000 miles on the clock, but replacing the valve cover gasket can be a solution.

The X5 E53 is fitted with expensive 'drainpipe' exhausts.

indicate sticking or worn brake pads). If the vehicle has covered over 150,000 miles, check that the handbrake shoes have been replaced; this should be detailed in the service history.

Newer X5 E53s (2004 and later), feature a helpful Condition Based

**18-inch alloy wheels on an X5 E53 –
one example of the 17 different wheels
available.**

Wheels/tyres   ④ ③ ② ①
There are 17 types of wheels to choose
from:

Ellipsoid styling – style 56
Measurements. . . . . 7,5 x 17
Tyres 235/65 R17

Star-spoke – style 57
Measurements. . . . . 7,5 x 17
Tyres 235/65 R17

Star-spoke – style 58
Measurements. . . . . 8,5 x 18
Tyres 255/55 R18H

V-spoke – style 63
Measurements. . . . . . 9 x 19 Front
10 x 19 Rear
Tyres 255/50 R19V
285/45 R19V

Star-spoke – style 69
Measurements . . . . 8,5 x 18
Tyres 255/55 R18H

Star-spoke – style 74
Measurements. . . . . 8,5 x 18
Tyres 255/55 R18H

Double-spoke composite wheel – style 75
Measurements. . . . . . 9 x 19 Front

10 x 19 Rear
Tyres 255/50 R19V
285/45 R19V

Star-spoke – style 87
Measurements. . . . . 9,5 x 20 Front
10,5 x 20 Rear
Tyres 275/40 R20W
315/35 R20W

Star-spoke – style 99
Measurements. . . . . 8 x 18
Tyres 255/55 R18H

V-spoke – style 130
Measurements. . . . . 7,5 x 17
Tyres 235/65 R17

Y-spoke – style 131
Measurements. . . . . 8,5 x 18
Tyres 255/55 R18

Star-spoke – style 132
Measurements. . . . . . 9 x 19 Front
10 x 19 Rear
Tyres 255/50 R19
285/45 R19

Individual V-spoke – style 152
Measurements. . . . . . 9 x 19 Front
10 x 19 Rear
Tyres 255/50 R19
285/45 R19

Star-spoke – style 153
Measurements. . . . . 8,5 x 18
Tyres 255/55 R18

V-spoke – style 168
Measurements. . . . . 9,5 x 20 Front
10,5 x 20 Rear
Tyres 275/40 R20W
315/35 R20W

Cross-spoke – style 177
Measurements. . . . . 9,5 x 20 Front
10,5 x 20 Rear
Tyres 275/40 R20W
315/35 R20W

Y-spoke – style 183
Measurements. . . . . 8,5 x 18
Tyres 255/55 R18

It has not been practical to take images of every wheel style, so, while you will find a selection throughout this book, the full variety can be viewed at: http://www.angelfire.com/biz7/bmwheelie/e53_wh.htm

Tyres ④ ③ ② ①

Tyres are a vital part of any vehicle. Brand new tyres are far safer than older, worn ones, because the tread on a new tyre enables a vehicle to brake to a halt much more quickly, particularly in wet conditions. Therefore, pay close attention to what tyres are on your prospective purchase, and ensure that they're correctly inflated. Invest a few pounds in a tread depth gauge – 1.6mm is the legal limit (in the UK) – any less and the tyres will need to be replaced.

Typically, your BMW X5 should be fitted with the following (although this is dependent on the size of wheels fitted as previously mentioned):

Front tyres: 235/50/18
Rear tyres: 245/45/18

Michelin Diamaris, Toyo Street Terrain, Pirelli, Marshalls and Bridgestones are all popular choices. Yokohama is considered a budget choice, wearing quicker due to the quality of the rubber.

Ultimately, though, driving style will govern how long tyres last. Bear in mind that the X5 is an all-wheel drive vehicle, so tyre wear should be uniform. If not, this will highlight a tracking or a balancing issue. Demanding driving will result in tyres not even lasting 15,000 miles, while more considerate driving will result in over 25,000 miles coverage.

Overall stance ④ ③ ② ①

While the X5 E53 uses one body, there are varying heights according to which model is purchased:

2000 to 2003 V8 67.2in (1707mm)
2001 to 2003 67.5in (1715mm)
2004 to 2006 V8 4.8i 67.9in (1725mm)
2004 to 2006 69.3in (1760mm)

No matter which model, they all have high ground clearance and a commanding position on the road, making for a capable off-roader. Overall ride height varies according to the wheels and tyres fitted, with slight differences being noticeable on differing suspension setups.

The ultimate Chelsea tractor.

Glass & wipers ④ ③ ② ①

Unfortunately, chipped and cracked windscreens are par for the course on a fast vehicle. That said, the X5 E53 is fortunate in that its ride height offers some protection for the windscreen from flying stones. Check the front and rear windscreens, side windows, wing mirrors and headlights for chips and cracks.

Windscreens, due to their size, are particularly susceptible. While a new windscreen or one that is in good

Windscreens can be expensive to replace, particularly if graduated-tinted or heated.

A new windscreen from Autoglass.

condition is a preferred choice, don't let a poor one put you off, because, once you've purchased fully comprehensive insurance, you should be able to get it repaired or even replaced for free or a minimal cost, usually without affecting your excess.

A replacement laminated green solar windscreen from Autoglass comes with a green shaded top tint. The windscreen is bonded to the body with removable trims. There is a fitting time of around 60 minutes, and the vehicle can be driven 60 minutes after bonding. Visit www.autoglass.co.uk

Windscreen measurements:

Width	1560(mm)
Thickness	0.00(mm)
Curvature	CD7723A
Height	900(mm)
Weight	14.50(kg)
Curvature depth	0(mm)

Rarely will side windows present a problem, but do check for scratches that might have resulted from driving too close to hedges and branches or from vandalism. The latter is a sad indictment of our society, and is often more likely to occur on the paintwork. Replacing side window glass will be costly because of the electrics involved. Wing mirror glass should be in its original state because these mirrors automatically fold in, thus protecting them. However, they can still pick up damage from driver error, for instance, clipping a parked car on driving past. It's important to check that the electric wing mirrors drop down when reversing, to help the driver see where he/she is going.

Check that there's rubber on the front and rear wiper blades. Windscreen wipers should be replaced every 12 months.

Body trim   [1]

Pick a fine day where there are good light levels and no rain.

A keen eye for detail is required when assessing the bodywork and trim. Start at the front, slowly making your way to the rear. Take your time, and don't feel pressured to hurry. If the seller tries to hurry you along, this should make you question whether he/she is trying to hide something.

Check the parking sensors on the front bumpers are intact and working.

In some respects the ride height of the X5 E53 can help protect the bodywork and trim from the sort of damage experienced by less tall vehicles, such as scratched bumpers from pavements, and/or parking damage. However, it is always possible to find examples that have been damaged through careless driving.

First and foremost, check the bumpers. Unless it has been rarely driven or re-sprayed there will be stone chips on the front bumpers, particularly from motorway driving. If it has been re-sprayed, has it been in an accident? Ask the owner for details. Is the bumper straight? If not it's likely to have been refitted following an accident. If you remain dissatisfied, commission an HPI (Hire Purchase Information) check (www.hpi.co.uk). This will either confirm or allay any suspicions (for a small fee).

Cast your eyes over every millimetre of paintwork, as you would when washing it, and you'll see any blemishes, bubbles, scratches, signs of re-spray, repairs and filler marks.

As you look down each side question whether the colour remains consistent. Are the doors/panels a slightly lighter/darker shade to each other? Do the doors fit perfectly or is there a slight gap or difference in height between the trim on one door compared to the others? Differences here could

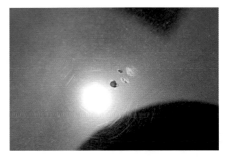

The appearance of unsightly stone chips can be improved by careful polishing – with T-Cut, for example.

Signs of re-spray: ill-fitting bumpers and paint overlap on black trim.

Rust is never an obvious issue on the bodywork of the BMW X5 E53, but plastic trim can hide it.

Check all external door handles work correctly – they are known to break.

As with the front bumper, check that the rear parking sensors are present and functioning.

suggest that a new door has been fitted following an accident. Are there any ripples along the doors or panels? If so, this could suggest that filler has been used. There's no door trim on the X5 E53, and the attractive aluminium running boards fitted to many were in fact optional extras. If fitted, check that they are a secure fit.

Check that the door handles work well, as these are known to seize, particularly if subjected to frost and ice.

Looking at the rear bumper, assess the colour. Is it consistent with the rest of the vehicle? Any cracks mean that it has been in a shunt. If it's in perfect condition, is it straight? Does it flow into the rear panels without any gaps? Are

there any tell-tale re-spray signs – paint marks where there shouldn't be, for instance.

Lighting

Halogen headlights are standard, while xenon high intensity discharge (Hid) lamps are optional, the latter giving excellent visibility whilst driving at night. X5s fitted with xenon headlights have automatic headlight adjustment control for varying loads. Headlight bulbs are replaced at the back of the headlight assembly. Pay particular attention to front and rear indicators, lights, the centre brake light, the light on the lower tailgate, and the number plate bulb. Check for malfunctioning.

Here's looking at you, kid: Check the lights work. These are xenon headlights.

Rear lights.

Headlights

Due to their position the front headlights are especially susceptible to chips and cracks. Do the headlights work – do they dip and work on full beam? Do the side lights work? Usually, any problems with the lights will be down to bulbs needing to be replaced, rather than needing entire new units.

If headlights need to be replaced, they cost several hundred ●. Front fog lights fitted into the bumper are cheaper to replace.

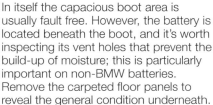

The front headlights complement the striking BMW double-kidney grille and badge.

Boot

In itself the capacious boot area is usually fault free. However, the battery is located beneath the boot, and it's worth inspecting its vent holes that prevent the build-up of moisture; this is particularly important on non-BMW batteries. Remove the carpeted floor panels to reveal the general condition underneath.

Is there any damage that may have been caused by a rear-end impact? Ensure all the electrics are dry, tidy and intact. Pull the retractable security cover back and forth to make sure that it operates smoothly.

The battery resides under the spare wheel in the boot. Is it in good condition, and is it the correct size and power for the X5 E53?

Operate the retractable security cover in the boot, making sure it's not broken or torn.

Underside, sills
& floors

In most cases damp can destroy. Your mission is to hunt it out. It is acceptable for a small amount of moisture to be present on axle and pulley seals because the leaking fluid helps the seal work correctly, but do look for minor fluid leaks. Experience will tell.

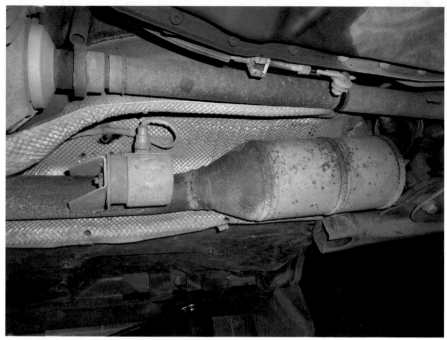

BMW X5 E53s originally benefited from a six-year limited anti-corrosion warranty requiring periodic checks. Expect corrosion if there has been no further treatment.

Have anti-corrosion sprays been used? If so, wax- or tar-based anti-corrosion compounds are the correct choice and in no circumstances should oil-based compounds be used, because they're incompatible with factory applied protection.

Fuel tank & pipework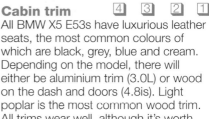

The saddle-shaped 93-litre (24.6gal) plastic fuel tank resides in the centre of the vehicle underneath the rear seat. The older plastic gets the more likely it is to crack and rupture; replacement can be necessary every ten years or so. If possible, it's worthwhile inspecting the fuel tank (by removing the rear seat, but it is strongly advised that an expert in such matters is contacted), which comprises the fuel pump, fuel level reading units, and suction jet pump. Attached to the fuel tank are fuel lines connecting the emissions control system and expansion tank. If the fuel filter has not been regularly changed, the fuel lines may need to be replaced due to the build-up of deposits.

The large fuel tank lies beneath the rear seat.

Cabin trim

All BMW X5 E53s have luxurious leather seats, the most common colours of which are black, grey, blue and cream. Depending on the model, there will either be aluminium trim (3.0L) or wood on the dash and doors (4.8is). Light poplar is the most common wood trim. All trims wear well, although it's worth bearing in mind that wood veneer can crack if subjected to long periods of hot weather. The leather trim is hard-wearing, although inevitably the driver's seat will suffer. Sagging leather, especially around the lumbar area, is a sure sign of a high-miler, while worn carpet in the footwell will confirm this impression. Some X5 E53s will have specialist oversized front seats with huge headrests fitted, providing greater support and comfort. The centre

Aluminium door and dashboard trim found in the X5 E53 3.0.

Make sure the inside door handles work.

console armrest can suffer from scuffing and discolouration. If there is veneered trim around the gear lever, this can be prone to damage. Check for flush and neat fitting trim, and that there are no unsightly marks or scuffs to any of the upholstery. Do the internal door handles work well? These are known to fail and are expensive to replace. X5 E53s have become well-known for having flimsy interior trim that does not last the course, including buttons and switches that break. So, if superglue doesn't work, it will have to be replaced professionally, which will be costly.

Run your hands along all the carpets, especially near the doors. They should be bone dry. If they are not the door seals could have broken. It is a fairly simple process to replace them and a competent fitter should do it fairly quickly and inexpensively.

Instruments & electrics

4 3 2 1

Assuming all the checks were carried

out during the fifteen minute evaluation, it's again worth checking that the switches and gauges work properly. Start with the electric window controls. All four windows feature one-touch operation in both directions. Holding the key in the unlock or lock position will open or shut the windows and sunroof. A circular switch above the window switches on the driver's trim operates the electric door mirrors. The power folding wing mirrors can be problematic as they get older, and are expensive to repair. However, depending on the problem, the following website does provide a free fix:

http://www.xoutpost.com/bmw-sav-forums/x5-e53-forum/46978-x5-folding-mirrors-problem.html

Check that the controls for the wing mirrors work; they should adjust and fold.

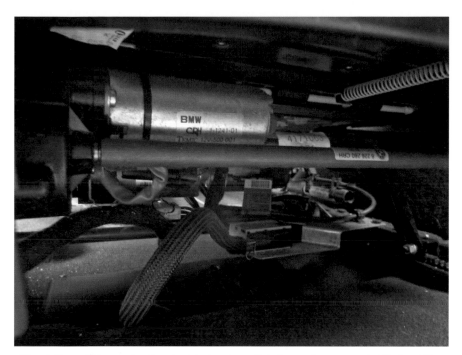

Check the cabling under the electric front seat(s), depending on model. It should be tidy and in good order.

On the entry level 3.0i model only the driver's seat is electrically operated. Both front seats are electric as standard on the other models. Ensure that the memory functions and all electrics work correctly. No error lights or messages should appear on the dash. The steering column is electrically-adjustable for length and height, and it's very important that this function works correctly. The steering wheel is adjusted by the seat and mirror memory function.

Check that all interior lighting works, and look closely at the centre console area. It is prone to lighting problems as well as function issues with the radio and television. If, for instance, the traction control light and ABS (Anti-lock Braking System) lights are on and will not switch off, then you should be warned that rewiring could be needed,

Spend time familiarising yourself with the complicated centre console.

perhaps due to a water leak in the rear battery compartment.

Of particular importance, if for no other reason than cost, is the television, which will not work correctly if the anti-theft code has not been input. If it is missing it could cost a few thousand pounds to get working. Check the CD player, as these are notoriously temperamental – often the 'on' switch fails. Pay attention to the OBC (On Board Computer), which is known for automatically switching itself on and off. As with all things electric, it's also common for the satellite navigation to stop working the older it gets, and so it's critical that you drill down into any issues the current owner has experienced. With a bit of luck you could be presented with a well-maintained model where issues have been resolved as they have occurred, rather than left to fester.

All X5 E53s are fitted with air-conditioning, and this should work quietly, quickly bringing down the temperature. Try the system at various temperature settings to ensure it works. Check that the PDC (Park Distance Control) works, because if this needs replacing it will be expensive.

Listen to the premium entertainment system and ensure that all the speakers work. Turn them up high to expose any rattling or tinny vibrations, a sure sign that they need replacing (a costly exercise, even if buying cheaper non-BMW types).

Check the amplifier, speakers, door speaker, door window frame speaker, rear door midrange speaker, dashboard speaker, and sub-woofers.

The optional CD changer is behind the left compartment panel in the boot.

Miscellaneous

Check the following, otherwise extra costs can be just round the corner:

• Are there two sets of keys and key

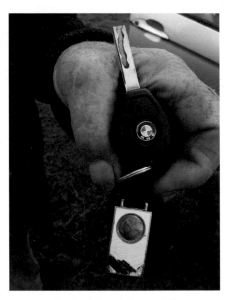

Do both key fobs work?

fobs? Do you know the security code for the TV/audio system?

• The sophisticated keyless remote access system incorporates a high-tech radio transmitter inside the X5 E53 key. This locks and unlocks the doors and tailgate by remote control. There's no need to ever replace this battery, as it is cleverly recharged while the key is in the ignition.

• Is all the paperwork present? Handbook, service record, security booklet, and any extra equipment handbooks (ie satellite navigation).

• Check in the boot that all the tools (such as the locking wheel nut key) are present and correct.

Test drive

Select drive mode on the five-speed automatic gearbox and it should smoothly change between gears with no jerkiness. At this point it is advisable to check the handbrake, too. If it's fairly stiff this is usually a sign of a well-maintained vehicle (unless it hasn't been driven for some time and the brakes have actually seized!).

Ensure that you drive the X5 both on and off road. You should find that the automatic gearbox is a pleasure to use, smoothly changing between gears, with sport mode providing that extra punch. This automatic can be also used as a manual.

A good driving position and a commanding view of the road make the X5 an ideal vehicle for overtaking, particularly on challenging roads. Its blue xenon headlights are particularly helpful for night-time driving, and these automatically switch on and level themselves.

There is rear privacy glass, and the cavernous boot is ideal for carrying awkward loads. When reversing, the electric wing mirrors should drop down to help the driver see where he/she is going, while the parking sensors provide an audible alert to obstacles behind.

Evaluation procedure

Add up the total points. Score: 84 = excellent; 63 = good; 42 = average; 21 = poor.

X5 E53s scoring over 59 will be completely usable and will require only maintenance and care to preserve condition. X5 E53s scoring between 21 and 43 will require some serious work (at much the same cost regardless of score). X5 E53s scoring between 44 and 58 will require very careful assessment of the necessary repair/restoration costs in order to arrive at a realistic value.

Check all the switches work on the electrically adjustable front seat(s) because this is vital to a good driving position.

10 Auctions
– sold! Another way to buy your dream

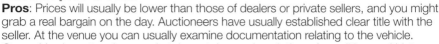

Auction pros & cons
Pros: Prices will usually be lower than those of dealers or private sellers, and you might grab a real bargain on the day. Auctioneers have usually established clear title with the seller. At the venue you can usually examine documentation relating to the vehicle.
Cons: You have to rely on a sketchy catalogue description of condition and history. The opportunity to inspect is limited, and you cannot drive the car. Auction cars are often a little below par and may require some work. It's easy to overbid. There will usually be a buyer's premium to pay in addition to the auction hammer price.

Which auction?
Auctions by established auctioneers are advertised in car magazines and on the auction houses' websites. A catalogue, or a simple printed list of the lots for auctions might only be available a day or two ahead, though often lots are listed and pictured on auctioneers' websites much earlier. Contact the auction company to ask if previous auction selling prices are available, as this is useful information (details of past sales are often available on websites).

Catalogue, entry fee and payment details
When you purchase the catalogue of the vehicle in the auction, it often acts as a ticket allowing two people to attend the viewing days and the auction. Catalogue details tend to be comparatively brief, but will include information such as 'one owner from new, low mileage, full service history,' etc. It will also usually show a guide price to give you some idea of what to expect to pay, and will tell you what is charged as a 'buyer's premium.' The catalogue will also contain details of acceptable forms of payment. At the fall of the hammer an immediate deposit is usually required, the balance payable within 24 hours. If the plan is to pay by cash there may be a cash limit. Some auctions will accept payment by debit card. Sometimes credit or charge cards are acceptable, but will often incur an extra charge. A bank draft or bank transfer will have to be arranged in advance with your own bank as well as with the auction house. No car will be released before all payments are cleared. If delays occur in payment transfers then storage costs can accrue.

Buyer's premium
A buyer's premium will be added to the hammer price: don't forget this in your calculations. It's not usual for there to be a further state tax or local tax on the purchase price and/or on the buyer's premium.

Viewing
In some instances it's possible to view on the day, or days before, as well as in the hours prior to, the auction. There are auction officials available who are willing to help out by opening engine and luggage compartments, and to allow you to inspect the interior. While the officials may start the engine for you, a test drive is out of the question. Crawling under and around the car as much as you want is permitted, but you can't suggest that the car you're interested in be jacked up, or attempt to do the job yourself. You can also ask to see any documentation available.

Bidding

Before you take part in the auction, decide your maximum bid – and stick to it! It may take a while for the auctioneer to reach the lot you're interested in, so use that time to observe the bidders. When it's the turn of your car, attract the auctioneer's attention and make an early bid. The auctioneer will then look to you for a reaction every time another bid is made, usually the bids will be in fixed increments until the bidding slows, when smaller increments will often be accepted before the hammer falls. If you want to withdraw from the bidding, make sure the auctioneer understands your intentions – a vigorous shake of the head when he/she looks to you for the next bid should do the trick!

Assuming you're the successful bidder, the auctioneer will note your card or paddle number, and, from that moment on, you will be responsible for the vehicle.

If the car is unsold, because it failed to reach the reserve or because there was little interest, it may be possible to negotiate with the owner, via the auctioneers, afterwards.

Successful bid

There are two more items to think about. How to get the car home, and insurance. If you can't drive the car, your own or a hired trailer is one way, another is to have the vehicle shipped using the facilities of a local company. The auction house will also have details of companies specialising in the transfer of cars.

Insurance for immediate cover can usually be purchased on site, but it may be more cost-effective to make arrangements with your own insurance company in advance, and then call to confirm the full details.

eBay and other online auctions?

eBay and other online auctions could land you a car at a bargain price, though you'd be foolhardy to bid without examining the car first, something most vendors encourage. A useful feature of eBay is that the location of the car is shown, so you can narrow your choices to those within a realistic radius of home. Be prepared to be outbid in the last few moments of the auction. Remember, your bid is binding, and it will be very, very difficult to get restitution in the case of a crooked vendor fleecing you!

Some cars in online auctions may be 'ghost' cars. Ensure the car actually exists and is as described (usually pre-bidding inspection is possible) before parting with your cash.

Auctioneers

Barrett-Jackson www.barrett-jackson.com/
Bonhams www.bonhams.com/
British Car Auctions (BCA) www.british-car-auctions.co.uk/
Cheffins www.cheffins.co.uk/
Christies www.christies.com/
Coys www.coys.co.uk/
eBay www.ebay.com/
H&H www.classic-auctions.co.uk/
RM www.rmauctions.com/
Shannons www.shannons.com.au/
Silver www.silverauctions.com/
Southampton Motor http://www.southamptonmotorauction.com/
South West Vehicle http://www.swva.co.uk/

Wally Pickett, from Shedfield in Hampshire, bought his BMW X5 at auction.

11 Paperwork
– correct documentation is essential

The paper trail
Classic, collector and prestige cars usually come with a large portfolio of paperwork accumulated and passed on by a succession of proud owners. This documentation represents the real history of the car, and from it can be deduced the level of care the car has received, how much it's been used, which specialists have worked on it, and the dates of major repairs and restorations. All of this information will be priceless to you as the new owner, so be very wary of cars with little paperwork to support their claimed histories.

MoT certificate.

Registration documents
All countries/states have some form of registration for private vehicles, whether it's like the American 'pink slip' system or the British 'log book' system.

It's essential to check that the registration document is genuine, that it relates to the car in question, and that all the vehicle's details are correctly recorded, including chassis/VIN and engine numbers (if these are shown). If you're buying from the previous owner, his or her name and address will be

MoT logo.

recorded in the document: this will not be the case if you're buying from a dealer.

In the UK the current (Euro-aligned) registration document is named 'V5C,' and is printed in coloured sections of blue, green and pink. The blue section relates to the car specification, the green section has details of the new owner, and the pink section is sent to the DVLA in the UK when the car is sold. A small section in yellow deals with selling the car within the motor trade.

In the UK, the DVLA will provide details of previous keepers of the vehicle upon payment of a small fee, and much can be learned in this way.

If the car has a foreign registration there may be expensive and time-consuming formalities to complete. Do you really want the hassle?

Roadworthiness certificate
Most country/state administrations require that vehicles are regularly tested to prove that they are safe to use on the public highway and do not produce excessive emissions. In the UK that test (the 'MoT') is carried out at approved testing stations, for a fee. In the USA the requirement varies, but most states insist on an emissions

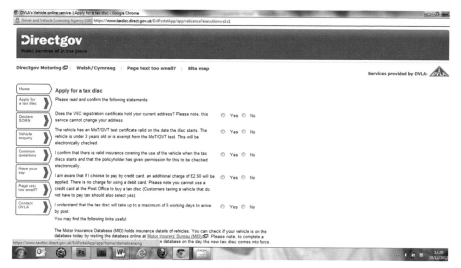

Road tax can now be purchased online.

test every two years as a minimum, while the police are charged with pulling over unsafe-looking vehicles.

In the UK the test is required on an annual basis once a vehicle becomes three years old. Of particular relevance for older cars is that the certificate issued includes the mileage reading recorded at the test date and, therefore, becomes an independent record of that car's history. Ask the seller if previous certificates are available. Without an MoT the vehicle should be trailered to its new home, unless you insist that a valid MoT is part of the deal. (Not such a bad idea, as at least you will know the car was roadworthy on the day it was tested and you don't need to wait for the old certificate to expire before having the test done.)

Road licence

The administration of every country/state charges some kind of tax for the use of its road system, the actual form of the 'road licence,' and how it is displayed, varying enormously country-to-country and state-to-state.

Whatever the form of the 'road licence,' it must relate to the vehicle carrying it, and must be present and valid if the car is to be driven on the public highway legally. The value of the license will depend on the length of time it will continue to be valid.

In the UK, if a car is untaxed because it has not been used for a period of time, the owner has to inform the licensing authorities, otherwise the vehicle's date-related registration number will be lost and there will be a painful amount of paperwork to get it re-registered.

Certificates of authenticity

Although perhaps not quite the case at the moment, what follows may be relevant in a few years. For many makes of collectible car it's possible to get a certificate proving the age and authenticity (eg engine and chassis numbers, paint colour and trim) of a particular vehicle, these are sometimes called 'Heritage Certificates,' and, if the car comes with one of these it is a definite bonus. If you want to obtain one, the relevant owners' club is the best starting point.

If the car has been used in European classic car rallies it may have a FIVA (Federation Internationale des Vehicules Anciens) certificate. The so-called 'FIVA Passport,' or 'FIVA Vehicle Identity Card,' enables organisers and participants to recognise whether or not a particular vehicle is suitable for individual events. If you want to obtain such a certificate go to www.fbhvc.co.uk or www.fiva.org. There will be similar organisations in other countries, too.

Valuation certificate

Hopefully, the vendor will have a recent valuation certificate, or letter signed by a recognised expert stating how much he, or she, believes the particular car to be worth (such documents, together with photos, are usually needed to get 'agreed value' insurance). Generally, such documents should act only as confirmation of your own assessment of the car rather than a guarantee of value, as the expert has probably not seen the car in the flesh. The easiest way to find out how to obtain a formal valuation is to contact the owners' club.

Service history

Often these cars will have been serviced at home by enthusiastic (and hopefully capable) owners for a good number of years. Nevertheless, try to obtain as much service history and other paperwork pertaining to the car as you can. Naturally, dealer stamps, or specialist garage receipts score most points in the value stakes. However, anything helps in the great authenticity game, items like the original bill of sale, handbook, parts invoices, and repair bills, adding to the story and the character of the car. Even a brochure correct to the year of the car's manufacture is a useful document and something that you could well have to search hard to locate in future years. If the seller claims that the car has been restored, then expect receipts and other evidence from a specialist restorer.

If the seller claims to have carried out regular servicing, ask what work was completed, when, and seek some evidence of it being carried out. Your assessment of the car's overall condition should tell you whether the seller's claims are genuine.

**They might look in tiptop condition,
but do the power wing mirrors
actually work?**

12 What's it worth?
– let your head rule your heart

Condition

If the car you've been looking at is really bad, then you've probably not bothered to use the marking system in chapter 9 – 60 minute evaluation. You may not have even got as far as using that chapter at all!

If you did use the marking system in chapter 9 you'll know whether the car is in Excellent (maybe Concours), Good, Average or Poor condition, or, perhaps, somewhere in-between these categories.

Many car magazines run a regular price guide. If you haven't bought the latest editions, do so now and compare their suggested values for the model you're thinking of buying: also look at the auction prices they're reporting. Values have been fairly stable for some time, but some models will always be more sought-after than others. Trends can change too. The values published in the magazines tend to vary from one magazine to another, as do their scales of condition, so read carefully the guidance notes they provide. Bear in mind that a vehicle in absolutely pristine condition could be worth more than the highest scale published. Assuming that the car you have in mind is not in show/concours condition, then relate the level of condition that you judge the car to be in with the appropriate guide price. How does the figure compare with the asking price? Before you start haggling with the seller, consider what affect any variation from standard specification might have on the car's value.

If you are buying from a dealer, remember there will be a dealer's premium on the price.

For UK prices check Parkers (www. parkers.co.uk), while the Kelley Blue Book (www.kbb.com) covers the USA.

Desirable options/extras

Metallic paint
Leather trim
Air-conditioning
Automatic climate control system
Multi-zone climate control
Front passenger's power seat
Heated front seats

Buyers like big wheels – they range from 17-inch to 20-inch – the larger the better.

Tastefully-finished X5 E53s hold their value well.

Cruise control
Navigation system
Sunroof
CD autochanger
Xenon headlamps
Tinted glass
17-inch alloy wheels
18-inch alloy wheels
19-inch alloy wheels
20-inch alloy wheels

Undesirable features

Money does not necessarily bring with it taste, and it has been known for BMW X5 E53s to suffer from garish makeovers that might be eye-catching but actually damage the future resale price of the vehicle. That owner of the bright orange example with leopard skin interior, take note. To complete the package, if a vulgar private numberplate is added, that's a sure fire way to further damage

the reputation of both the vehicle and its owner. But it takes more than that to damage the Intimidator, as coined by the respected motoring hack Honest John. An LPG (Liquid Petroleum Gas) conversion, for instance. It might seem a good idea to fit this in order to halve fuel

Fancy having a Calor gas tank inside your vehicle? No thanks.

bills but it will dramatically hamper performance and make you look a laughing stock at the traffic lights. Not just that, these conversions impinge on boot or spare wheel space. There are increasingly common stories of botched installations, too, that result in car fires. If considering a vehicle that has been subjected to this conversion, it's absolutely imperative that a reputable installer was used – make sure there is supporting documentation. Hardly surprising then that owners steer well clear of these conversions.

Striking a deal
Negotiate on the basis of your condition assessment, mileage, and fault rectification cost. Also take into account the car's specification. Be realistic about the value, but don't be completely intractable: a small compromise on the part of the vendor or buyer will often facilitate a deal at little real cost.

Don't forget to check the spare wheel. One in good condition such as this shows a caring owner.

13 Do you really want to restore?

– it'll take longer and cost more than you think

Do you fancy saving up to 25 per cent on a used X5 E53?

Of course you do, but the catch is that it'll be a Category D write-off.

Don't be put off by the term 'write-off,' though, because in this context it should refer to the fact that the insurance company has written-off the vehicle in a financial sense rather than the vehicle being a physical write-off.

Category D write-offs are vehicles that have suffered light accident damage. Perhaps the X5 E53 requires light bodywork repairs, or the airbags have been triggered needing replacement costing a few thousand pounds. These are vehicles that would cost less to repair than their value.

Consider this example: a used X5 E53 worth £15,000 is involved in a minor collision. An insurer might have to pay for it to be towed to an approved repairer and then for subsequent storage costs. An assessor would be sent out to inspect the damage. The owner might have to hire a car incurring extra cost. Then there's personal injury claims, too.

It is, therefore, far easier for the insurance company to simply write-off the X5 E53, getting up to 65 per cent of its value from a salvage company, which then gets it repaired far cheaper at an independent dealer or sells it on to a buyer to repair.

This X5 E53 at Fab Direct in Gloucester has a blown engine and so will have a much lower resale value.

Unfortunately, some X5 E53s are just too far gone to repair, although they may still be useful for parts.

Graham Threlfall, the head of the National Association of Bodyshops, says: "Ten years ago, if a vehicle was involved in a front-end collision, the damage was confined to the bodywork, but with airbags, belt tensioners and equipment like self-levelling headlamps, it is much more expensive to repair them now. Insurers are often happier to do away with the liability."

Well-repaired Category D X5 E53s can appeal to budget-conscious buyers, but when they sell it on they must let the buyer know its history. A good source of accident-damaged BMW X5 E53s is FAB Recycling Ltd in Gloucester, www.fabdirect.com.

According to the Office of Fair Trading, all reasonable steps to check a vehicle's history, including whether it's been written-off, should be taken by dealers before selling any vehicle.

Graham Threlfall, head of the National Association of Bodyshops.

14 Paint problems
– bad complexion, including dimples, pimples and bubbles

Paint faults generally occur due to lack of protection/maintenance, or to poor preparation prior to a re-spray or touch-up. Some of the following conditions may be present in the car you're looking at:

Orange peel
This appears as an uneven paint surface, similar to the appearance of the skin of an orange. The fault is caused by the failure of atomized paint droplets to flow into each other when they hit the surface. It's sometimes possible to rub out the effect with proprietary paint cutting/rubbing compound or very fine grades of abrasive paper. A re-spray may be necessary in severe cases. Consult a bodywork repairer/paint shop for advice on the particular car.

Cracking
Severe cases are likely to have been caused by too heavy an application of paint (or filler beneath the paint). Also, insufficient stirring of the paint before application can lead to the components being improperly mixed, and cracking can result. Incompatibility with the paint already on the panel can have a similar effect. To rectify the problem, it's necessary to rub down to a smooth, sound finish before re-spraying the problem area.

Crazing
Sometimes the paint takes on a crazed rather than a cracked appearance when the problems mentioned under 'Cracking' are present. This problem can also be caused by a reaction between the underlying surface and the paint. Paint removal and re-spraying the problem area is usually the only solution.

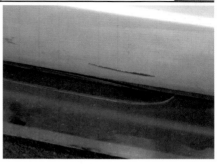
Scuffed and scratched bumpers are a sign of neglect.

A stone chip has rusted on a BMW X5 E53.

Blistering
Almost always caused by corrosion of the metal beneath the paint. Usually perforation will be found in the metal, and the damage will usually be worse than that suggested by the area of blistering. The metal will have to be repaired before repainting.

Micro blistering
Usually the result of an economy re-spray where inadequate heating has allowed moisture to settle on the car before spraying. Consult a paint specialist, but usually damaged paint will

A scratched driver's door on a BMW X5 E53.

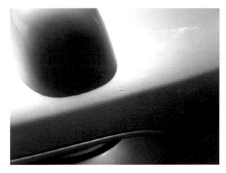

Stone chips on the front bumper of a BMW X5 E53.

As rubber ages it gets lighter in colour, but it is possible to revive it with a replenishing product from manufacturers such as Auto Glym and Armor All.

Black metal trim around the windows can become discoloured and weather beaten. This can be remedied by a good shampoo and polish.

have to be removed before partial or full re-spraying. Can also be caused by car covers that don't 'breathe.'

Fading

Some colours, especially reds, are prone to fading if subjected to strong sunlight for long periods without the benefit of polish protection. Sometimes proprietary paint restorers and/or paint cutting/rubbing compounds will retrieve the situation. Often a re-spray is the only real solution.

Peeling

Often a problem with metallic paintwork when the sealing lacquer becomes damaged and begins to peel off. Poorly applied paint may also peel. The remedy is to strip and start again!

Dimples

Dimples in the paintwork are caused by the residue of polish (particularly silicone types) not being removed properly before re-spraying. Paint removal and repainting is the only solution.

Dents

Small dents are usually easily cured by the 'Dentmaster,' or equivalent process, that sucks or pushes out the dent (as long as the paint surface is still intact). Companies offering dent removal services usually come to your home: consult your telephone directory.

15 Problems due to lack of use
– just like their owners, X5s need exercise!

Cars, like humans, are at their most efficient if they exercise regularly. A run of at least ten miles, once a week, is recommended.

Seized components
Pistons in calipers, slave and master cylinders can seize.

The clutch may seize if the plate becomes stuck to the flywheel because of corrosion.

Handbrakes (parking brakes) can seize if the cables and linkages rust.

Pistons can seize in the bores due to corrosion.

Fluids
Old, acidic, oil can corrode bearings.

Uninhibited coolant can corrode internal waterways. Lack of antifreeze can cause core plugs to be pushed out, even cracks in the block or head. Silt settling and solidifying can cause overheating.

Brake fluid absorbs water from the atmosphere and should be renewed every two years. Old fluid with a high water content can cause corrosion and pistons/calipers to seize (freeze), and can cause brake failure when the water turns to vapour near hot braking components.

Tyre problems
Tyres that have had the weight of the car on them in a single position for some time will develop flat spots, resulting in some (usually temporary) vibration. The tyre walls may have cracks or (blister-type) bulges, meaning new tyres are needed. Tyres fitted to old alloy wheels can deflate if the alloy wheels are corroded. Flat tyres can also be the result of a leaky valve.

A severe tyre and alloy wheel problem.

Shock absorbers (dampers)
With lack of use, the dampers will lose their elasticity or even seize. Creaking, groaning and stiff suspension are signs of this problem.

Rubber and plastic
Radiator hoses may have perished and split, possibly resulting in the loss of all coolant. Window and door seals can harden and leak. Gaiters/boots can crack. Wiper blades will harden.

Electrics
The battery will be of little use if it has not been charged for many months.

Earthing/grounding problems are common when the connections have corroded.

Sparkplug electrodes will often have corroded in an unused engine.

Insulation can harden and fail.

Rotting exhaust system
Exhaust gas contains a high water content so exhaust systems corrode very quickly from the inside when the car is not used.

A corroded underside is to be expected, although it will be even more severe if the vehicle has had little use.

A cared for X5 will have covers on the tyre valves.

– key people, organisations and companies in the X5 world

Clubs, organisations, forums and magazines

UK owners' club
PO BOX 328
Melksham
Wiltshire
SN12 6WJ
Telephone: 01225 709009
Web: http://www.bmw.co.uk/bmwuk/owner/car_club/
 http://www.bmwcarclubgb.co.uk/
Email: bmwcarclub@btconnect.com

The BMW Club
Brian Johnson
Web: http://www.thebmwclub.org.uk/
Email: marketing@bmwclub.org.uk

US owners' club
http://www.bmw-x5.net/
Email: info@bmw-x5.net

International clubs
Free to join: http://www.bmwownersclub.com/forums/index.php/forum/14-bmw-x5-series-club/
http://e53club.ru/
http://www.bmwclub.ru/bmw/x5.php

Forums
http://bmwenthusiasts.co.uk
http://www.facebook.com/pages/BMW-X5-AND-X6-Clubs-Europa/166636593397890
http://www.facebook.com/pages/BMW-X5-Fun-Club/84495740935

Accident-damaged X5 E53s provide a good source of good quality used parts.

http://www.bimmerfest.com/forums/
showthread.php?t=586107
http://www.bmwland.co.uk/forums/
viewforum.php?f=24
http://x5mclub.com/forums/
http://www.bmwccgbforum.co.uk/x5-
fuel-consumption_topic2078.html

BMW X5 specialists and parts suppliers

UK

Bartley Independent BMW Specialists
Unit 23 24 New Forest Enterprise
Centre
Rushington Business Park
Chapel Lane
Southampton
Hampshire
SO40 9LA
Tel: 02380 661 499
enquiries@bartleyuk.com
http://www.bartleyuk.com/

FAB Recycling Ltd
Broadmoor Road
Cinderford
Gloucestershire
GL14 2YL
Tel: 01594 827333
Web: http://www.fabdirect.com

Grosvenor Motor Company Limited
Independent BMW Specialists
10 Richfield Avenue
Reading, Berkshire. RG1 8EQ
Tel: 0118 958 3481
info@bmwspecialistsreading.co.uk
http://bmwspecialistsreading.co.uk

LK Spares (Specialist BMW Breakers)
16-17 Horsecroft Place
Pinnacles
Harlow
Essex CM19 5BU
Tel: 01279 417755
Email: enquiries@bmspares.co.uk
http://www.bmspares.co.uk

Specialist Cars Stevenage

Gunnels Wood Road,
Stevenage, Hertfordshire, SG1 2BE
Tel: 0845 539 0072
http://www.specialistcarsbmw.co.uk

USA
Andy's Autosport
United States
Tel: 1800 419 1152
http://www.andysautosport.com

West Coast Motorsport – customised
car specialist delivering unique cars
anywhere in the world
Tel: 866 853 1968
sales@westcoastmotosport.com
http://www.westcoastmotorsport.com

Parts suppliers
Carparts4less
Tel: 0845-6030607
Email: custservice@carparts4less.co.uk
Web: http://www.carparts4less.co.uk

Modifications and upgrades
Kudos Automotive Limited
Unit 2 Hunters Lane Industrial Estate
Rugby CV21 1EA
Tel: 01788 567 567
http://www.kudosbmw.co.uk

Chip Express
CHIP Express
UNIT 8 – The Gavel Centre
Porters Wood
St Albans
Hertfordshire
AL3 6PQ
Tel: 01727 730 956
http://www.chipexpress.com

Useful information sources
BMW Car Magazine
Unity Media Plc
Becket House
Vestry Road
Sevenoaks
Kent TN14 5EJ
Tel: 01732 748000

Fax: 01732 748001
Email: bmwcar@unity-media.com
Web: http://www.bmwcarmagazine.com/

Total BMW Magazine
Email: webmaster@kelsey.co.uk
Web: http://www.total-bmw-mag.co.uk/

Performance BMW Magazine
Unity Media Plc

Becket House
Vestry Road
Sevenoaks
Kent
TN14 5EJ
Tel: 01732 748000
Email: pbmw@unity-media.com
http://www.performancebmwmag.com/

BMW Tuning Magazine
Web: http://www.bmwtuningmag.com/

Don't be seduced by an attractive rear. The wiper on this example is ill-fitting and too close to the lower edge of the screen.

17 Vital statistics
– essential data at your fingertips

Production figures
BMW X5 (E53 and E70) over one million vehicles produced since 1999.

Technical specifications
Minor changes took place throughout the production period of the vehicles.
3.0i M54 engine, 6-cylinder – 170kW (228hp) @ 5900rpm
4.4i M62 TU engine, V8 – 210kW (282hp) @ 5700rpm
4.4i N62 engine, V8 (Valvetronic) – 210kW (282hp) @ 5400rpm
4.6is M62 TU engine, V8 – 255 kW (342hp) @ 5700rpm
4.8is N62 engine, V8 (Valvetronic) – 294kW (394hp) @ 6600rpm

Transmissions
Manual 5-speed S5D280Z
Manual 6-speed GS637BZ
Automatic 5-speed A5S390R
Automatic 5-speed A5S440Z
Automatic 6-speed GA6HP26Z

Dimensions
Length: 183.7in, 466.598cm or 4666mm (six inches shorter than a BMW 5-series)
Width: 73.7in, 187.198cm or 1871.98mm (a BMW 7 series measures 1800mm)
Height: 67.2in, 170.688cm or 1706.88mm, although some models vary
Weight: 2170kg, 4784lb

Suspension
Front: MacPherson strut wishbone (some models can have air springs)
Rear: MacPherson strut wishbone (some models can have air springs)

Brakes
All round discs and pads, power assisted with ABS

Steering
Variable power assisted and pinion with adjustable steering wheel

Wheels
17 types of wheel to choose from, ranging from 17-inch to 20-inch

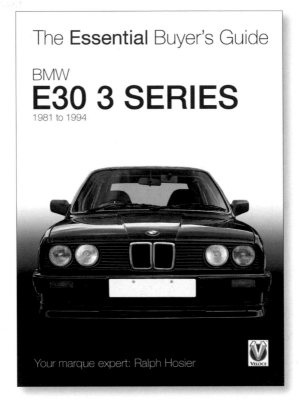

Also from Veloce Publishing –

The Essential Buyer's Guide™ series ...

| 978-1-845840-22-8 | 978-1-845840-26-6 | 978-1-845840-29-7 | 978-1-845840-77-8 | 978-1-845840-99-0 | 978-1-904788-70-6 | 978-1-845841-01-0 | 978-1-845841-07-2 |

| 978-1-845841-19-5 | 978-1-845841-13-3 | 978-1-845841-35-5 | 978-1-845841-36-2 | 978-1-845841-38-6 | 978-1-845841-46-1 | 978-1-845841-47-8 | 978-1-845841-61-4 |

| 978-1-845841-63-8 | 978-1-845841-65-2 | 978-1-845841-88-1 | 978-1-845841-92-8 | 978-1-845842-00-0 | 978-1-845842-04-8 | 978-1-845842-05-5 | 978-1-845842-31-4 |

| 978-1-845842-70-3 | 978-1-845842-81-9 | 978-1-845842-83-3 | 978-1-845842-84-0 | 978-1-845842-87-1 | 978-1-84584-134-8 | 978-1-845843-03-8 | 978-1-845843-07-6 |

| 978-1-845843-09-0 | 978-1-845843-16-8 | 978-1-845843-29-8 | 978-1-845843-30-4 | 978-1-845843-34-2 | 978-1-845843-38-0 | 978-1-845843-39-7 | 978-1-845843-40-3 |

£9.99 - £12.99 / $19.95
(prices subject to change, p&p extra).

The **Essential** Buyer's Guide

Ford
RS Cosworth
Sierra & Escort

All models 1985 to 1996

Your marque expert:
Dan Williamson

VELOCE PUBLISHING
THE PUBLISHER OF FINE AUTOMOTIVE BOOKS

Other books from Veloce Publishing's The **Essential** Buyer's Guide

Alfa Romeo Giulia GT Coupé (Booker)
Alfa Romeo Giulia Spider (Booker)
Audi TT (Davies)
Austin Seven (Barker)
Big Healeys (Trummel)
BMW E21 3 Series (1975-1983) (Reverente)
BMW E30 3 Series 1981 to 1994 (Hosier)
BMW GS (Henshaw)
BMW X5 (Saunders)
BSA 500 & 650 Twins (Henshaw)
BSA Bantam (Henshaw)
Citroën 2CV (Paxton)
Citroën ID & DS (Heilig)
Cobra Replicas (Ayre)
Corvette C2 Sting Ray 1963-1967 (Falconer)
Ducati Bevel Twins (Falloon)
Ducati Desmodue Twins (Falloon)
Ducati Desmoquattro Twins - 851, 888, 916, 996, 998,
    ST4 1988 to 2004 (Falloon)
Fiat 500 & 600 (Bobbitt)
Ford Capri (Paxton)
Ford Escort Mk1 & Mk2 (Williamson)
Ford Mustang – First Generation 1964 to 1973 (Cook)
Ford RS Cosworth Sierra & Escort (Williamson)
Harley-Davidson Big Twins (Henshaw)
Hinckley Triumph triples & fours 750, 900, 955, 1000,
    1050, 1200 – 1991-2009 (Henshaw)
Honda CBR FireBlade (Henshaw)
Honda CBR600 Hurricane (Henshaw)
Honda SOHC Fours 1969-1984 (Henshaw)
Jaguar E-Type 3.8 & 4.2-litre (Crespin)
Jaguar E-type V12 5.3-litre (Crespin)
Jaguar Mark 1 & 2 (All models including Daimler
    2.5-litre V8) 1955 to 1969 (Thorley)
Jaguar S-Type – 1999 to 2007 (Thorley)
Jaguar X-Type – 2001 to 2009 (Thorley)
Jaguar XJ-S (Crespin)
Jaguar XJ6, XJ8 & XJR (Thorley)
Jaguar XK 120, 140 & 150 (Thorley)
Jaguar XK8 & XKR (1996-2005) (Thorley)
Jaguar/Daimler XJ 1994-2003 (Crespin)
Jaguar/Daimler XJ40 (Crespin)
Jaguar/Daimler XJ6, XJ12 & Sovereign (Crespin)
Kawasaki Z1 & Z900 (Orritt)
Land Rover Series I, II & IIA (Thurman)

Land Rover Series III (Thurman)
Lotus Seven replicas & Caterham 7: 1973-2013
    (Hawkins)
Mazda MX-5 Miata (Mk1 1989-97 & Mk2 98-2001)
    (Crook)
Mercedes Benz Pagoda 230SL, 250SL & 280SL
    roadsters & coupès (Bass)
Mercedes-Benz 280-560SL & SLC (Bass)
MG Midget & A-H Sprite (Horler)
MG TD, TF & TF1500 (Jones)
MGA 1955-1962 (Crosier)
MGB & MGB GT (Williams)
MGF & MG TF (Hawkins)
Mini (Paxton)
Morris Minor & 1000 (Newell)
New Mini (Collins)
Norton Commando (Henshaw)
Peugeot 205 GTI (Blackburn)
Porsche 911 (964) (Streather)
Porsche 911 (993) (Streather)
Porsche 911 (996) (Streather)
Porsche 911 Carrera 3.2 (Streather)
Porsche 911SC (Streather)
Porsche 924 – All models 1976 to 1988 (Hodgkins)
Porsche 928 (Hemmings)
Porsche 930 Turbo & 911 (930) Turbo (Streather)
Porsche 944 (Higgins)
Porsche 986 Boxster (Streather)
Porsche 987 Boxster & Cayman (Streather)
Rolls-Royce Silver Shadow & Bentley T-Series (Bobbitt)
Subaru Impreza (Hobbs)
Triumph Bonneville (Henshaw)
Triumph Herald & Vitesse (Davies)
Triumph Spitfire & GT6 (Baugues)
Triumph Stag (Mort)
Triumph Thunderbird, Trophy & Tiger (Henshaw)
Triumph TR6 (Williams)
Triumph TR7 & TR8 (Williams)
Vespa Scooters – Classic 2-stroke models 1960-2008
    (Paxton)
Volvo 700/900 Series (Beavis)
VW Beetle (Cservenka & Copping)
VW Bus (Cservenka & Copping)
VW Golf GTI (Cservenka & Copping)

www.veloce.co.uk

First published in September 2013 by Veloce Publishing Limited, Veloce House, Parkway Farm Business Park, Middle Farm Way, Poundbury,
Dorchester, Dorset, DT1 3AR, England.
Fax 01305 250479/e-mail info@veloce.co.uk/web www.veloce.co.uk or www.velocebooks.com.
ISBN: 978-1-845845-26-1 UPC: 6-36847-04526-5
British Library Cataloguing in Publication Data – A catalogue record for this book is available from the British Library.
Typesetting, design and page make-up all by Veloce Publishing Ltd on Apple Mac. Printed in India by Replika Press.

A legend of road and track – Moonstone Blue Sierra RS500 Cosworth is the rarest of the rare.

Few cars can truly claim to be legends in their own lifetimes. Yet the RS Cosworth became a household name the moment it appeared in Ford showrooms during 1986.

A real racer for the roads, the RS Cosworth was developed with the sole aim of scooping international competition success – a task it achieved so well that, within a few years, it was outlawed by motorsport governing bodies.

Originally designed for touring car racing, the Sierra RS Cosworth was created under regulations that required Ford to build 5000 production models.

Its secret was a two-litre, turbocharged engine, created by Cosworth Engineering to produce over 300bhp in race form. It was mated to a hefty rear-wheel drive transmission, then dropped into a three-door Sierra bodyshell that boasted a functional bodykit and enormous rear wing for high-speed stability. Its plush spec included a smart interior with sporty Recaro seats.

Although the Cosworth engine was detuned to 204bhp for road-going versions, its 149mph performance was staggering. Its reputation as a supercar slayer was instant, and awestruck enthusiasts nicknamed it the Cossie.

Meanwhile, tuners took advantage of the incredible engine, doubling its standard power without making any major mechanical modifications.

Of course, Ford was already one step ahead. To keep winning races, the Sierra RS500 Cosworth was born. It gained a stronger engine plus revised suspension and extra aerodynamic aids. Motorsport rules meant 500 road cars were produced – all based on regular November 1986-built RS Cosworths, converted to RS500 guise during 1987.

Although the standard RS500 pumped out 224bhp, track versions made 550bhp-plus. The RS500 became the most successful touring car racer of all time, and the Cossie's place in history was secured.

But Ford couldn't waste such an amazing formula. In 1988 the three-door's mechanicals were wrapped into a sophisticated four-door package using the Sierra Sapphire Ghia body. Two years later, it gained a four-wheel drive transmission and strengthened powerplant to create the Sierra Sapphire RS Cosworth 4x4.

Ford's plan was to make a competitive rally machine, thus the 4x4's running gear and tweaked engine – including shortened floorpan and inner wings – were transplanted into a reworked Mk5 Escort bodyshell, using 50 per cent all-new panels and an even more dramatic whale-tail spoiler.

Competition eligibility required 2500 production examples, but the Escort continued in production until 1996. Several guises were offered – including standard, Motorsport and Luxury specs – plus a Monte Carlo limited edition and, from 1994, the last of the Cosworth line. Known colloquially as the small-turbo Escort Cosworth, it contained revisions to aid practicality – notably a reduced-size turbocharger for improved throttle response.

Eventually, sales dried up; emissions laws, theft risks and crippling insurance costs were all to blame.

But despite the RS Cosworth's demise, its desirability remains strong among thrill-seeking motorists. Some increase their cars' performance to four times the standard power, many polish their prized investments, and others simply enjoy using them as everyday drivers.

Whatever your intention, there's an RS Cosworth to suit your needs; and this book, we hope, will help you to find that perfect Cossie.

Thanks
Huge thanks to everyone who helped to get this book together, especially Paul Linfoot at North Yorkshire RS Spares for his expert advice, and Jamie King at *Fast Ford* magazine for fact-checking and his endless enthusiasm for rusty old Sierras.

Contents

The Essential Buyer's Guide™ currency
At the time of publication a BG unit of currency "●" equals approximately
£1.00 (US$1.54/Euro 1.16). Please adjust to suit current exchange rates
using Sterling as the base currency.

RS Cosworths offer a sporty driving position with fabulous low-slung Recaro seats. This is the three-door/RS500 cabin.

Tall and short drivers
Plenty of headroom and seat travel for tall or short drivers, with a height-adjustable driver's seat on all models.

Weight of controls
Although RS Cosworths were built (and are still useable) as everyday cars, the gearbox and clutch may feel heavy to drivers more familiar with modern front-wheel-drive hatchbacks. But these cars are sporty and precise, with sharp power-assisted steering and turbo lag that suddenly leaves you holding tight on take-off!

Will it fit in the garage?
Length: Sierra 175.5in (4458mm); Sapphire 176.9in (4494mm); Escort 165.8in (4211mm).
Width: Sierra 68in (1727mm); Sapphire 66.8in (1697mm); Escort 68.3in (1734mm).
Height: Sierra and Sapphire 54.2in (1377mm); Escort 56.1in (1425mm).

Interior space
All Cosworths were closely based on family cars, so interior space is perfectly adequate – even by modern standards.

Luggage capacity
Sierras have loads of boot space, and all are capacious when the back seat is folded flat (a useful feature on all models, including Sapphire).
Sierra: 24.4cu ft (690 litres)
Sapphire: 14.6cu ft (413 litres)
Escort: 9.4cu ft (267 litres)

Running costs
RS Cosworths were never cheap to run, and they're getting more expensive with age. Servicing (although reasonably priced) must be regular, breakages are common, parts can be pricey and fuel consumption is heavy – especially with engine modifications and a bit of fun behind the wheel ...

Usability
Completely practical on a daily basis (unless highly modified) – but thieves are still a real danger.

Parts availability
New components are becoming harder to find (especially body parts and trim) but virtually everything's out there at a price, and most bits are readily available secondhand. Uprated components are often a sensible (sometimes expensive) solution.

Many parts are shared with regular Fords, but some – like the RS500's twin rear spoilers – are extremely rare and expensive.

Parts cost
Parts shared with standard Fords are cheap and cheerful, but anything with an RS or Cosworth badge carries a massive premium – which unfortunately applies to most of the spares you'll need!

Insurance
Limited mileage and cherished insurance policies are available for reasonable costs. Even highly-modified Cosworths are perfectly insurable, although it's wise to emphasise security precautions.

Investment potential
RS500 prices are already high, but standard, unmolested three-doors and Escorts may continue to climb. Immaculate Sapphires can only increase.

Alternatives
BMW M3, Mercedes 190E 2.3/2.5-16, Mitsubishi Lancer Evolution, Nissan Skyline GTR/S, Subaru Impreza Turbo, Vauxhall Cavalier/Calibra Turbo.

2 Cost considerations
– affordable, or a money pit?

Purchase price
Buy cheap, pay twice. An old cliché, maybe, but it perfectly sums up Cosworth ownership.

Purchasing a tired, tatty example is an inexpensive way to get behind the wheel of a fast, iconic car, but you'll almost certainly spend just as much bringing it back to health.

Similarly, splashing out on expensive components and tuning upgrades may seem frivolous, yet could save cash compared to ploughing money into low-end accessories that don't work properly, wear out quickly, and potentially cause lasting damage elsewhere.

Finally, bear in mind the so-called Cosworth tax – an automatic price hike for anything RS-related, even if it's a standard Sierra or Escort part.

Parts prices (new reproduction parts)
Head gasket ●x50
Cam cover gasket ●x18
Clutch kit ●x140
Brake pads (front) ●x29
Brake discs (front) ●x48
Steering rack (recon) ●x200
Front wing, Sierra ●x100
Front wing, Sapphire ●x60
Sill, Sierra ●x60
Battery tray, Escort ●x30
Rear lamp, Escort ●x32

A working Cosworth YB engine is always worth good money – just add zeroes if you want more power.

Parts prices (secondhand – prices can vary enormously depending on condition and spec)
Standard crankshaft ●x500
RWD engine, with ancillaries ●x1500
4x4 engine, with ancillaries ●x2000
ABS pump ●x70
Front bumper, three-door ●x400
Front bumper, RS500 ●x2000
Driver's seat, three-door ●x200
Dashboard, three-door ●x1000
Rear bumper, Sapphire ●x100
Header tank, RWD ●x300
Turbo heat shield, Escort ●x150
Centre console, Escort ●x150
Orange indicator lenses, three-door/
  Escort ●x75

Front indicators are unique to the Sierra and Escort Cosworth.

If you're looking for an easy ride, you might be best advised to keep away from anything wearing an RS Cosworth badge.

That's not to say all Cosworths are unreliable money pits. Yes, they are uncompromising, uncivilised, harsh, noisy, getting old and likely to have led hard lives. And if a Cosworth decides to go wrong, it could be an expensive experience.

But RS Cosworths are iconic high-performance machines. They're fast, fun, look great and can seat a full family in comfort. And with an enthusiastic following plus an impending classic car status, all are appreciating assets.

Although a standard Cosworth doesn't sound especially powerful by today's standards, it's nevertheless packing over 200bhp in a lightweight package (a three-door weighs only 1205kg), with little provision for safety or driver aids.

Okay, every car has effective anti-lock brakes, but there are no airbags (except on the very last Escorts) and no traction control. Also, with loads of turbo lag (it feels like nothing's happening when you accelerate, then the turbo suddenly kicks in and the car surges forward), a Cosworth can be a handful in the hands of a beginner – especially a beginner who's more familiar with front-wheel drive machinery.

Rear-wheel-drive Cosworths (Sierras and early Sapphires), in particular, can catch out the unwary. Although the chassis gives great feedback, if you lose concentration when pressing on – especially in wet weather – a RWD machine can bite hard, shooting you off the road ... backwards.

In contrast, the 4x4 setup (later Sapphires and all Escorts) has huge amounts of grip, meaning immense point-to-point performance and an all-round easier drive. It comes at the expense of fun; the 4x4 feels woollier behind the wheel, lacking the rear-drive's livelier feeling through the throttle and ability to slide at will.

Nevertheless, a Cosworth can be an accomplished cross-country performer or motorway mile-muncher – if you can accept the alarming fuel consumption of a race-bred sports machine when used to its full potential. Cruising off-boost allows the Cosworth engine to behave almost like a normal car, but when the turbocharger's working hard it's sucking in huge quantities of fuel. Needless to say, most modifications accentuate the gas guzzling, while stop-starting around town isn't exactly the Cosworth's natural environment ...

Still, a properly-functioning clutch pedal is easy to press, and all Cosworths have highly-responsive power-assisted steering as standard. Only the gearchange may feel awkward at first; if you're more accustomed to modern cars, you could be surprised by the Cosworth's positive (if agricultural) shift.

Every Cosworth has a comfortable, enthusiast-focused cockpit, including sporty driving position and figure-hugging

Leather-equipped Sapphire brings luxury for back-seat passengers.

With such a dynamic appearance, even a plain white Escort Cosworth will command attention.

Recaro seats, often trimmed in durable grey cloth. Many Sapphires and Luxury-spec Escorts were also offered with optional Raven (dark grey/black) leather upholstery, which extended to the rear seats.

Talking of which, don't forget all Cosworths were based on run-of-the-mill Ford family cars, so each will accommodate five adults. What's more, boot space is impressive throughout the range, and each car is practical to use every day.

The biggest worry with regular use is the risk of theft; in their heyday, RS Cosworths were renowned for being stolen, and insurance premiums still reflect the fact. A good security system should help, but don't forget that bewinged monsters (three-doors and most Escorts) attract huge amounts of attention from the public; if you want to keep a low profile in a Cosworth, only the Sapphire's minicab-like bodywork may slip by unnoticed. A late Escort with deleted aeropack might just about manage, too, but don't bet on it …

Of course, you'll also need to bear in mind the Cosworth's requirement for regular maintenance. Tyres, brakes and clutches wear quickly; rust is a constantly nagging worry, and frequent servicing is a must – preferably by a Cosworth specialist rather than your usual garage. Even when new, Ford main dealers often shied away from Cosworths, and genuine parts dried up years ago. Despite their outward similarity to regular Sierras and Escorts, most mechanicals are completely different, and trim is incredibly difficult to source.

Sadly, a neglected Cosworth can be a financial liability, and thanks to their time in the secondhand market, thousands of Cosworths have been bought cheaply, tuned on low budgets, thrashed mercilessly, smashed into the scenery, stolen, bodged, and broken up for spares.

That's left a minefield of a secondhand market, where concours, low-mileage Cosworths mix with tired, tatty examples, and cars that have been rebuilt or modified to incredible levels.

Would you wish to keep the car standard, or tweak the turbocharged engine to its full potential? Although factory-original show machines are becoming collectable, upgrading a Cosworth is an addictive habit that can double (or even quadruple) standard output to produce an amazing road or track weapon. The downside is that getting sucked into the upgrades game could cost more than your house did …

Whichever Cosworth you choose, you're guaranteed a machine with legendary status and fantastic ability. Get a good one, and it's an unforgettable drive. The Cosworth ownership experience simply shouldn't be missed.

RS Cosworths are equally at home on road or track. Anywhere, in fact, as long as they're being driven hard.

Simply stunning! An Imperial Blue Escort RS Cosworth will always attract an army of would-be buyers.

Are you looking for an RS Cosworth to drive and enjoy, or simply stash away as a gold-lined investment? The car you choose could depend on your plans, but may also be determined by how much cash you can afford to spend.

The RS500 is now a serious collector's piece, with ever-increasing values that mean modifications or regular use will have a detrimental effect. For an almost identical look, feel and ownership experience, a regular RS Cosworth three-door will fit the bill – and, at less than half the price, may be driven to its full potential whenever you please.

Escorts tend to fall into three categories – show machines, ultra-modified monsters and scruffy secondhand motors. It's easy to choose depending on your intentions, but bear in mind it will cost less to buy any pre-modified Cosworth than adapt a standard car.

Sapphires are available for the least money, due to their large production numbers and less-glamorous looks. Arguably the most driveable of all Cosworths (especially in RWD form), their values can only increase – although current low prices mean many have been neglected, so may be tattier as a result.

Rear-wheel-drive Sierra Sapphire is fast, fun and extremely capable – yet four-door Cossie prices are lowest of all.

Values
RS500 100%
Sierra three-door 40%
Escort 30%
Sapphire 20%

5 Before you view
– be well informed

To avoid a wasted journey, and the disappointment of finding that the car does not match your expectations, it will help if you're very clear about what questions you want to ask before you pick up the telephone. Some of these points might appear basic, but when you're excited about the prospect of buying your dream Cosworth, it's amazing how some of the most obvious things slip the mind ... Also check car magazines and websites for the current values of the model you are interested in, which give price guides and auction results.

Where is the car?
Is it going to be worth travelling to the next county/state, or even across a border? A locally advertised car, although it may not sound very interesting, can add to your knowledge for very little effort, so make a visit – it might even be in better condition than expected.

Dealer or private sale?
Establish early on if the car is being sold by its owner or by a trader. A private owner should have all the history, so don't be afraid to ask detailed questions. A dealer may have more limited knowledge of a car's history, but should have some documentation. A dealer may offer finance and a warranty/guarantee (ask for a printed copy), providing more of a comeback if that pricey RS turns out to be a fake.

Cost of collection and delivery
A dealer may well be used to quoting for delivery by car transporter. A private owner may agree to meet you halfway, but only agree to this after you have seen the car at the vendor's address to validate the documents. Conversely, you could meet halfway and agree the sale but insist on meeting at the vendor's address for the handover.

View – when and where?
It is always preferable to view at the vendor's home or business premises. In the case of a private sale, the car's documentation should tally with the vendor's name and address. Arrange to view only in daylight and avoid a wet day; most cars look better in poor light or when wet.

Reason for sale?
Do make it one of the first questions. Why is the car being sold and how long has it been with the current owner? How many previous owners? Bear in mind many Cosworths have had several drivers seeking a temporary thrill, so keep your judgement reserved.

Left-hand drive to right-hand drive/specials
If a steering conversion has been done it can only reduce the value and it may well be that other aspects of the car still reflect the specification for a foreign market. Very few Cosworths have been converted, though, so it's not a big worry. But remember, no road-going RS500s were built with left-hand drive.

Condition (body/chassis/interior/mechanicals)
Ask for an honest appraisal of the car's condition. Ask specifically about some of the check items described in chapter 7.

All original specification?
An original equipment car is invariably of higher value than a customised version. But Cosworths with documented and well-executed mechanical modifications may command a decent premium, and approved adaptations for competitive motorsport sometimes have a positive effect.

Matching data/legal ownership
Do VIN/chassis, engine numbers and licence plate match the official registration document? Is the owner's name and address recorded in the official registration documents?

For those countries that require an annual test of roadworthiness, does the car have a document showing it complies (an MoT certificate in the UK, which can be verified on 0845 600 5977)?

If a smog/emissions certificate is mandatory, does the car have one?

If required, does the car carry a current road fund license/licence plate tag?

Does the vendor own the car outright? Money might be owed to a finance company or bank: the car could even be stolen. Several organisations will supply the data on ownership, based on the car's licence plate number, for a fee. Such companies can often also tell you whether the car has been 'written-off' by an insurance company. In the UK these organisations can supply vehicle data:
HPI – 01722 422 422
AA – 0870 600 0836
DVLA – 0870 240 0010
RAC – 0870 533 3660
Other countries will have similar organisations.

Unleaded fuel
All Cosworth heads have hardened valve seats, but only green- or blue-top engines will run on normal unleaded (when standard). All others require at least 97 RON (super unleaded) petrol or suitable octane booster.

Insurance
Check with your existing insurer before setting out; your current policy might not cover you to drive the car if you do purchase it. The word Cosworth still strikes fear into the hearts of some insurers!

How you can pay?
A cheque/check will take several days to clear and the vendor may prefer to sell to a cash buyer. However, a banker's draft (a cheque issued by a bank) is as good as cash, but safer, so contact your own bank and become familiar with the formalities that are necessary to obtain one.

Buying at auction?
If the intention is to buy at auction see chapter 10 for further advice.

Professional vehicle check (mechanical examination)

There are often marque/model specialists who will undertake professional examination of a vehicle on your behalf. Owners' clubs will be able to put you in touch with such specialists.

Other organisations that will carry out a general professional check in the UK are:
AA – 0800 085 3007 (motoring organisation with vehicle inspectors)
ABS – 0800 358 5855 (specialist vehicle inspection company)
RAC – 0870 533 3660 (motoring organisation with vehicle inspectors)
Other countries will have similar organisations.

6 Inspection equipment
– these items will really help

This book
Reading glasses (if you need them for close work)
Magnet (not powerful, a fridge magnet is ideal)
Torch
Probe (a small screwdriver works very well)
Overalls
Mirror on a stick
Digital camera
A friend, preferably a knowledgeable enthusiast

Before you rush out of the door, gather together a few items that will help as you work your way around the car. This book is designed to be your guide at every step, so take it along and use the check boxes to help you assess each area of the car you're interested in. Don't be afraid to let the seller see you using it.

Take your reading glasses if you need them to read documents and make close-up inspections.

A magnet will help you check if the car is full of filler, or has fibreglass panels. Use the magnet to sample bodywork areas all around the car, but be careful not to damage the paintwork. Expect to find a little filler here and there, but not whole panels. There's nothing wrong with fibreglass panels, but a purist might want the car to be as original as possible.

Take real care when lifting a Cosworth – jacking in the wrong place can flatten the floorpan or cause the bodyshell to flex.

A torch with fresh batteries will be useful for peering into the wheelarches and under the car.

A small screwdriver can be used – with care – as a probe, particularly in the wheelarches and on the underside. With this you should be able to check an area of severe corrosion, but be cautious – if it's really bad the screwdriver might go right through the metal!

Be prepared to get dirty. Take along a pair of overalls, if you have them. Fixing a mirror at an angle on the end of a stick may seem odd, but you'll probably need it to check the condition of the underside of the car. It will also help you to peer into some of the important crevices. You can also use it, together with the torch, along the underside of the sills and on the floor.

If you have the use of a digital camera, take it along so that later you can study some areas of the car more closely. Take a picture of any part of the car that causes you concern, and seek a friend's opinion.

Ideally, have a friend or knowledgeable enthusiast accompany you: a second opinion is always valuable. Owners' clubs are great places to ask for help.

7 Fifteen minute evaluation
– walk away or stay?

General condition

Before getting stuck in to a thorough inspection, a Cosworth needs a quick assessment – there's much to be learned from taking a step back and getting a good overall view.

First, does it look like an honest, genuine car? Is it sitting evenly on the road? Is the paintwork original, or recently repaired? Are there any obvious rust spots or signs of damage? Has the car been modified? Is it pretending to be something it's not?

And what about the owner's attitude? Cosworths need plenty of maintenance, but has the seller cared for the car properly? Do they polish it every weekend, or thrash it mercilessly from cold?

Regardless of how immaculate the car appears, don't forget most Cosworths have led hard lives. Keep your eyes open, and assume there are bad bits bubbling beneath the surface.

Bodywork

Rust is the biggest killer of any old Ford, and the Cosworth is no exception. Although its European build quality was better than British Sierras (but only just), it's crucial to inspect any prospective purchase for serious rot.

Most obvious will be the rear wheelarches, which can corrode through the inner arches, rear wings and into the cabin. Door bottoms go too, rusting from the edges, up the skins and around the windows.

Inspect the engine bay, looking for corrosion and cracks around the bulkhead, battery tray and suspension turrets.

Rust is your enemy – it's vital to inspect the inner wings, chassis and sills for signs of corrosion.

Get underneath and examine the crossmember and front chassis rails for rust or ripples. Feel around the floorpan for rot, especially in the sills under the side skirts. Most importantly, check the rear chassis box sections, which can corrode badly.

Check the front wings are original; they should feature neat seam sealer where they join the slam panel, which should also be home to the VIN tag and body colour plate. If not, chances are the front end's suffered a prang. Let's be honest: Cosworths are high-powered sports saloons, and plenty have been involved in accidents at the hands of drivers blessed with more bravery than skill. Be on guard for off-shade paintwork, overspray or creases. Stand back and check the panel gaps – they were never perfect from new, but particularly poor alignment points to an adverse history.

If you find a few minor faults, don't be put off. Cosworths are 20-odd-year-old fast Fords, so you can't expect perfection.

Interior

It shouldn't be a deal-breaker, but bear in mind a tatty Cosworth interior can cost

A tidy interior reflects well on a Cosworth's overall condition. Missing trim can be pricey to replace.

thousands to rectify. What's more, a tidy cabin is usually a good sign that the car has been well looked-after.

Most of the cockpit is standard Ford, so don't expect amazing durability. The dashboard could be cracked, especially along the top; good replacements are rare. The headlining may be sagging, and the seats could be worn – notably the driver's bolster.

Cosworth Recaros are unique to the model, trimmed in grey cloth or leather. Make sure the door cards match, and aren't torn; trim is prone to wrinkling and lifting away – which can be expensive to repair.

Service history

Before handing over any cash, it's wise to check a Cosworth's service history. While you can't really expect many examples to have a fully stamped-up main dealer service book, most are accompanied with a stack of receipts for maintenance needed to keep them in good shape.

Ideally, the receipts will be from a recognised RS specialist (generally a better sign than stamps from a Ford dealership) and they should relate to the car's current spec. If the owner's claiming a fresh, 450bhp engine, he should have paperwork to back it up.

At the very least, expect to see evidence of recent fluid swaps and cambelt change. Recommended intervals are up to 6000 miles for oil (fully synthetic), and 48,000 miles or four years for the cambelt; experts advise doing it sooner – straight away, if you can't guarantee the car's history.

Vehicle identification number (VIN)

Cosworths had a well-deserved reputation for being the UK's most stolen car, and today they're sometimes faked or reshelled. Above all else it's essential to check any car's identity.

First, ensure the chassis number on the car's V5 (don't even think about buying a Cosworth without a log book) matches its VIN plate (riveted neatly to the bonnet slam panel) and the number under the carpet flap between the driver's seat (RHD cars) and inner sill. Ideally, it shouldn't be surrounded by welding/grinding marks or filler, but sills often rot away, so don't immediately reject a car purely because it's been welded.

On road cars, the chassis number should start with WFOEXXGBBE (three-doors and RS500s), WFOFXXGBBF (Sapphires) or WFOBXXGKAB (Escorts), followed by two letters for the year and month of manufacture, then the car's unique five-digit ID.

Late Escorts also have an ID tag on the dashboard, visible through the lower nearside corner of the windscreen, repeating the chassis number.

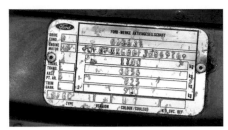

Your first check should be the VIN tag, found on the bonnet slam panel.

Chassis number is stamped into the offside sill beneath this flap in the carpet.

Lots more information is noted on the VIN tag, including engine code of N5, drive of B (for right-hand drive), trans is J or L (RWD) or 8 (4x4), and axle is 3 (RWD) or U (4x4).

If there's any doubt about dodgy numbers, be sure to invest in a history check – which is also essential for establishing the car's ownership and whether it's ever been written-off. Any more doubt, and run away. Fast.

Engine identity

At the heart of any RS Cosworth is its magnificent turbocharged powerplant, boasting an alloy 16-valve cylinder head, 1993cc capacity (in factory-standard form), and immense tuning potential.

Yet the YB's cylinder block was based on the regular Pinto unit found in millions of Fords worldwide, and some parts are even interchangeable. So it's essential to know what's under the bonnet.

Designated the YB series, the RS Cosworth's engine was manufactured in a variety of guises as production progressed. Three-door Sierras and rear-wheel-drive Sapphires received the 204bhp YBB, featuring a red cam cover and what's known as a 205 cylinder block, due to the large 205 cast onto the crankcase under the turbo and above the oil filter.

The strengthened YBD (found only in the RS500) also had a red top, along with better cylinder head (including larger inlet ports), eight-injector setup, big T4 turbo and

Huge power can be extracted from the Cosworth engine, but you'll ideally want receipts from a recognised specialist.

224bhp. Its cylinder block was strengthened, too: although marked 205 (reduced-size 205 cast onto the right-hand side just below the cylinder head), it had thicker walls and smaller core plugs than the usual YB items (⅞in diameter).

The early Sapphire 4x4 contained a YBJ; again, wearing a red cam cover. It also had revised gudgeon pin positions (designed to reduce piston slap from cold), and a stiffer cylinder block that was designated 200 thanks to '200' digits cast in place of the previous 205.

From 1990 the Sapphire was equipped with a YBG, now wearing a green cam cover plus catalytic converters. Early Escort Cosworths (known as 'big turbo' cars) had essentially the same motor, now called YBT, boasting 227bhp and a blue top. Small-turbo Escorts instead featured a YBP with all-new, smooth-finish, silver-painted cam cover.

Small-turbo Escorts benefited from countless other revisions internally and externally (including different core plug locations, improved cylinder head with larger ports, a new ignition system, ECU, manifolds, and so on).

You'll need to check a Cosworth has the correct cylinder block. A 200 block in an early car is generally acceptable, but not vice versa (the thinner 205 part isn't considered strong enough for the extra stresses of all-wheel-drive transmission). Similarly, a regular 205 block isn't recommended for much more than 400bhp, so start asking questions if a RWD Cosworth is claiming big power from its stock bottom end.

As for the RS500, to preserve originality (and value) it needs its proper YBD block.

YB engines have two unique identity numbers – one hand-stamped by Ford and another by Cosworth. Ford's should ideally match the VIN's final seven characters – you'll find it on a machined flat section just before the offside engine mount. Cosworth's number is stamped onto the front of the crankcase above the water pump, beginning with YBB, YBJ, YBG, YBT or YBP (depending on which version you're buying) followed by unique digits.

To make matters more complicated, RS500 engine numbers never match the VIN or V5: instead of a YBD designation, RS500 paperwork refers to the YBB of the regular three-door Cosworth on which each RS500 is based. Genuine RS500 numbers were YBD0015 to YBD0537.

Sierra RS Cosworth three-door identification

Based on a bottom-of-the-range Sierra 1.3 or 1.6 three-door body (rather than the XR4i's three-side-window shape), the original three-door RS Cosworth featured few factory-made alterations from the original shell.

Other than the obvious assets of a turbocharged YB engine, T5 gearbox, chunky drivetrain and bodykit (plus identity numbers), it's not easy to spot a fake or ringer. Here are some pointers for the real thing:
• Large transmission tunnel (bows out towards the front footwell).
• Straight towing eye.
• Inverted keyhole-shape cutout on the bulkhead behind the brake servo.
• Sunroof (road cars).
• No sunroof (Motorsport shells).
• Bonnet pressed for vent cutouts.
• No seam sealer (Motorsport shells).
• Colours: Diamond White, Moonstone Blue or Black.
• 170mph instruments with boost gauge.
• Electric front windows.

Sierra Sapphire RS Cosworth identification

Thanks to the model's popularity and relatively low value, fewer Sapphires have been faked or reshelled than three-doors. Nevertheless, it's essential to check any Cosworth is the proper thing. The Sapphire was based on a Ghia body, with the following features:

A glass sunroof should be present unless the car has a Motorsport bodyshell (supplied only in white).

• Large transmission tunnel (bows out towards the front footwell).
• Straight towing eye.
• Inverted keyhole-shape cutout on the bulkhead behind the brake servo.
• Sunroof (electric optional on 4x4).
• Bonnet pressed for vent cutouts (4x4).
• Chassis rail driveshaft cutouts (4x4).
• Colours (RWD) include: Diamond White, Crystal Blue, Mercury Grey, Magenta, Moonstone Blue, Flint Grey and Black.
• Colours (4x4) include: Diamond White, Magenta, Moonstone Blue, Flint Grey, Ebony Black, Moondust Silver, Smokestone Blue, Nouveau Red and Radiant Red.
• 170mph speedometer.
• Electric windows all-round (except some foreign markets).

Escort RS Cosworth identification

Although it looked like a Mk5 Escort, the RS Cosworth shared few body parts with lesser-models, and was in fact hand-built by Karmann using some Escort panels over a shortened Sierra 4x4 floorpan and inner wings. This makes replicating a car almost unheard of – although it's obviously wise to check what you're buying.

• Sunroof (electric optional on Luxury model).
• No sunroof (standard/Motorsport shells).
• No seam sealer (Motorsport shells).
• Colours (big-turbo) include: Diamond White, Radiant Red, Polaris Grey, Imperial Blue, Pacifica Blue, Black, Ash Black and Mallard Green.
• Colours (small-turbo) include: Diamond White, Ash Black, Radiant Red, Imperial Blue, Auralis Blue, Aubergine and Stardust Silver.
• Electric front windows (Luxury model).
• Opening rear side windows (Luxury model).

Escort RS Cosworth Monte Carlo identification

The Monte was a special edition run of 200 Escort RS Cosworths, produced in right-hand drive and left-hand drive.
• Colours: Mallard Green, Ash Black or Jewel Violet.
• Sunroof.
• Electric front windows.
• Monte decals on doors and tailgate.

Monte Carlo was a special-edition Escort RS Cosworth.

- OZ Racing 8x16in alloys.
- Raven cloth interior with Recaro and Motorsport logos.
- Chrome gearknob and handbrake button.
- Numbered plaque on dashboard.

RS500 identification

The most valuable RS Cosworth of all (other than genuine motorsport machines) is the Sierra RS500, so named due to its run of just 500 units (including four prototypes). All were based on pre-constructed RS Cosworth three-doors, which were subsequently converted to RS500 spec (before registration) by Tickford. All were road cars – RS500 racers were built from three-door Motorsport shells.
- VIN number between WFOEXXGBBE38600 and WFOEXXGBBE39099.
- YBD engine based on uprated 205 block.
- Engine number between YBD0015 and YBD0537, not corresponding with VIN number.
- Eight-injector inlet manifold and extra fuel rail (blanked off).
- Extra outlet from fuel pressure regulator.
- Larger throttle body (76mm rather than 60mm) with unique linkage.
- Unique alternator adjuster, map sensor bracket, turbo damper (horse-shoe-shaped) and heater pipework.
- Larger intercooler.
- T4 turbo.
- Right-hand drive.
- Unique trailing arm mounts.
- Colours: Diamond White (56 built), Moonstone Blue (52 built) or Black (392 built).
- Sunroof.
- Modified front bumper with enlarged air intake and vents in place of fog lamps (supplied in the boot) and unique front splitter.
- Modified whale tail with additional 30mm lip.
- Additional unique lower rear spoiler.
- Electric aerial in offside rear wing.

Note: no build number plaque was fitted by the factory.

When buying an RS500, ensure all its special components are present – including this eight-injector setup.

Modifications

Cosworth ownership and modifications are almost inseparable. So, unless you're looking for a concours factory-original show machine, don't be put off by a few enhancements – especially if it's just a stainless steel exhaust system, uprated dampers and modern tyres.

Engine upgrades can be a little more troublesome to examine prior to purchase. It's natural to find a chipped (remapped) engine ECU (after all, Cosworths were detuned by Ford for road use), along with beefier intercooler and bigger fuel injectors – such a spec can add over 100bhp to the factory-quoted figure, without overstressing the standard engine.

Large-scale power hikes can be a minefield, and if you're planning on 500bhp-plus (800bhp is feasible, if you've got deep enough pockets), you'll need to appreciate that there will be sacrifices in reliability, fuel consumption and usability.

The best advice when viewing any modified car is to ask to see receipts for the work involved – that way you can be sure it's been applied to a healthy engine by a recognised Cosworth specialist, rather than cheap, off-the-shelf add-ons to a smoky old high-miler.

Even something as simple as an ECU chip may be responsible for problems further down the line. Such basic, low-cost upgrades control the fuel, air and boost supplied to the engine, which may have dire consequences. Anything from poor idling and rough running, right up to component failure and a melted engine could be the result.

Modified Cosworths can be massive fun to drive on road or track, and a thoroughly addictive hobby. But don't expect upgrades to add much overall value to a vehicle, and don't be distracted by shiny paint or a glittering engine.

Tasteful modifications may add value, especially when as impressive as this Escort's big brakes and 18in alloys.

8 Key points
– where to look for problems

Rot spotting
Beware of Cossie corrosion. Cosworths rot through their inner wings, strut towers, chassis rails and sills, along with rust around the rear wheelarches, fuel cap, front wings, boot floor and more.

Look everywhere – especially beneath the car – for rust, splits, filler or fresh underseal.

It may cost thousands to return a car to top condition after years of neglect.

Neglect
A real Cossie killer, lack of maintenance can lead to all manner of problems – from tatty bodywork to complete engine meltdown. The current owner's attitude may display more cause for concern than hard evidence.

Chassis number is stamped into the offside floorpan alongside the driver's seat (RHD).

Crash damage
Many Cosworths have been involved in accidents, so check the car's history for crash damage, along with evidence of poor panel gaps, off-shade paintwork, overspray or creases in the floors, inner wings and chassis rails.

Identity
Above all, beware a stolen or faked Cosworth – there are loads around. Be suspicious of any car with a dubious registration (number or logbook), absent history, disguised identity tags or strange specification. Don't buy an RS500, in particular, without in-depth knowledge of its original kit.

Cosworth-specific trim – such as these three-door door cards – can be tricky and costly to replace.

Interior and trim
If they're missing or damaged, even a few bits of trim could cost thousands to replace. If you're paying top cash for a Cosworth, mug up on specs and check the interior is in tiptop condition.

RS Cosworths were magnets for car thieves, so be extra vigilant: a damaged door lock could be the least of your worries ...

Score each section as follows: 4 = excellent; 3 = good; 2 = average; 1 = poor
The totting up procedure is detailed at the end of the chapter. Be realistic in your marking!

Engine

The all-conquering Cosworth YB engine has its origins in the humble Pinto powerplant, so it's mainly straightforward.

But that's not to say you don't need to take extra care when buying. Today, few Cosworth engines remain standard (doubling the output is easy), parts can be alarmingly expensive (sometimes leading to neglect), and age has often taken its toll.

YBs cope remarkably well with high mileages – providing they've been well-treated. Evidence of a full service history is an obvious plus point.

Unless you're viewing a low-mileage museum piece, assume a Cosworth has undergone at least one engine rebuild. Even so, don't believe recent work automatically represents a clean bill of health – big power upgrades reduce life expectancy, some mechanical reconditioning is done to a poor standard, and owners occasionally tell fibs ... Besides, with a Cosworth there's always something to go wrong.

Once you're happy the engine has a genuine identity number rather than grinding marks, look at its overall appearance. A grotty engine bay suggests neglect: Cosworth cam covers may drip a little oil, but grime everywhere points to major leaks; if so, chances are it's not been serviced properly, and possibly been allowed to run low on oil, which can cause innumerable issues.

Talking of leaks, check for coolant running down the cylinder block, especially at the back on the exhaust side – it could be from a blown head gasket. Pay particular attention to rear-wheel drive cars, which had an inferior head design to 4x4s. Similarly, heavily-modified engines are prone, because excess turbo boost can be a head gasket killer.

Head gasket failure is costly, requiring cylinder head removal, testing and skimming; big problems arise when the head has suffered internal heat damage, or has already been skimmed excessively (138.6mm is the minimum with standard pistons) – the solution is a replacement cylinder head.

So don't forget the obvious checks for oily film in the coolant header tank or excessive creamy residue under the oil filler cap, bearing in mind a little could be condensation. Make sure the engine oil is nice and clean, too, without 'mayonnaise' on the dipstick.

Starting the engine is next, preferably from cold. Get an assistant to watch the exhaust pipe as it fires into life; check there's no blue smoke, which would likely be due to worn valve stem seals or turbo oil seals. Mild smoking at idle shouldn't be cause for concern (it's probably old or excessively thin oil), but great plumes warrant investigation.

White smoke (or steam) at idle should ring alarm bells, possibly pointing to turbo trouble or the aforementioned head gasket failure.

Meanwhile, if the car has an oil pressure gauge (standard in all Escort

Cosworths, while many Sierras have aftermarket dials), make sure it reads strongly when hot and cold.

Now is also the time to listen for nasty noises. The YB is pretty agricultural (naturally harsh and purposeful-sounding), so don't expect refinement.

Ticking from the top end is likely to be from tired cam followers – often just one or two tappets, but if they don't quieten when warm you'll need to replace all 16. Not cheap.

Knocking from lower down is usually nothing to worry about on a cold RWD engine, and should subside when the oil gets warm. The noise (which sounds similar to a typical diesel engine's rattle) is generally what's known as piston slap, and perfectly normal on 205-block YBs even when factory-fresh. Cosworth 4x4s have different pistons, which shouldn't knock at all (4x4 pistons are a direct fit into a RWD block, eliminating piston slap there, too). Hearing slap from 4x4 pistons is bad news, but not hearing it doesn't mean all is well – there's plenty more to go wrong!

Other knocking or rumbling sounds aren't so simple, and can be signs of an imminent wallet-emptying experience. Growling when a warm engine is revved could represent a damaged crankshaft, along with appropriately expensive rebuild costs.

The almighty Cosworth YB powerplant – seen here in all-conquering RS500 guise.

The small-turbo Escort Cosworth engine included numerous alterations.

A test drive is vital to inspect the engine's health. A Cosworth should feel strong, even by today's standards. If it doesn't, there's something wrong.

While listening for scary noises, look in the rear-view mirror at what's leaving the exhaust. A few puffs of blue smoke on the overrun are nothing to worry about, and don't be too concerned by a little mist under hard acceleration, especially if the car's been modified. Constant oil-burning and moderate-to-heavy blue smoke points to a piston problem (including rings or cylinder bores) or turbo trouble; the latter is the most likely culprit for smoke while driving on boost. Again, white clouds while driving probably mean head gasket failure.

Oh, and don't be surprised by black smoke from the exhaust, which will be the result of overfuelling. Although it's generally safer for the engine than running lean, it can cause major problems when excess petrol washes oil off the cylinder bores, in turn wrecking bottom end bearings.

Ignition system

   [1]

Misfires and Cosworths go hand in hand, with many potential causes – so listen for spluttering from the engine, and take a test drive using a variety of revs to feel for hesitation.

A stutter under acceleration could be something cheap and simple like tired, poor-quality HT leads or incorrectly-gapped sparkplugs. YBs are known for destroying plugs and requiring extra-tight plug gaps. It's also common for rocker cover gaskets to split, leading to poor running when engine oil drips into the plug holes.

Plug type can play a part. Using the wrong heat range can cause serious engine damage, particularly in small-turbo Escorts, which run dual coil packs under the cam cover. Coil packs and their wiring are prone to breakages, sometimes resulting in the car running on only two cylinders.

Cosworths and ignition trouble go hand-in-hand; coils are prone to failure.

Don't be surprised if a Cosworth needs new plugs and leads.

Unfortunately, most major coughing is hard to trace. All earlier Cosworths had a traditional ignition coil on the inner wing, which results in heavy misfires when it fails. Similarly, a variety of ignition components could be to blame, including the king lead, distributor cap or rotor arm.

If you're buying a Cosworth to use (rather than invest in), finding a car with a wasted spark conversion is a bonus. This system ditches the traditional coil-based affair (found on all Cosworths before the small-turbo Escort) in favour of a twin-coil setup without any troublesome moving parts. It's said to eliminate misfires and damp problems, so if these problems are still present, suspect other causes.

Electrical sensors and connections are possibilities, as are fuelling issues or bad tuning. But don't assume a hesitating Cosworth will be cheap or easy to fix. Remember, misfires may result from a blowing head gasket and/or cracked cylinder head, so stay on guard!

Turbo

It's thanks to a hefty turbocharger that the RS Cosworth makes so much power. But it's also to blame for pricey problems ...

Several different turbos were used throughout production. Stock RWD Sierras and Sapphires wore a Garrett T03, with a similar T03B on the 4x4. The RS500 contained a whopping T4, while early Escorts had a T3/T04B. A T25 was used on the last Escorts; thus the 'small-turbo' nickname. Many modified cars have uprated turbos, but all the essential checks remain relevant.

Begin with the engine switched off. Remove the intake hose from between the airbox and turbocharger inlet. Inspect the impellor, feeling the shaft for excessive front-to-rear movement, which means a tired turbo or impending failure: very slight play from side to side is okay, but sloppiness suggests worn bearings and turbo rebuild time.

If there's wet oil in the turbo housing it's likely the seals are blown. Similarly, sludge in the intercooler pipework is a warning sign.

Oh, and while you're there, examine the turbocharger damper, which could have sheared off.

Turbo trouble should be evident when taking a test drive. Again, check for smoke from the exhaust – big, blue clouds while driving on boost points to knackered turbo oil seals.

Fluctuating boost pressure can be a sign of trouble, so ensure it holds strong under hard acceleration. Three-doors and Escorts contain a boost gauge, and many Sapphires have an aftermarket dial, which makes checking much easier.

Don't be surprised if nothing happens under light throttle – Cosworths are renowned for turbo lag, and feel sluggish until the boost kicks in. That said, small-turbo Escorts get going from 2000rpm.

Air leaks are a common cause of boost problems – emanating from parts including split or loose boost hoses, sensors and regulators – but they're often awkward and time-consuming (read: expensive) to trace.

Boost issues can lead to fuelling troubles and the potential expense of complete engine failure, so be extra-vigilant of modified cars.

Remove the inlet hose and check inside the turbocharger.

Cooling system

Most of the Cosworth's cooling system is pretty basic (the water pump doesn't really give trouble, despite being a standard Sierra component), albeit with the addition of an intercooler.

There are a few things to watch out for, though, with head gasket failure the chief concern. Check there's no oily film in the header tank or thick, white sludge under the oil filler cap (if there's only a bit it could be from condensation).

With the engine running, you'll also need to look for white smoke from the exhaust, bubbles in the header tank, and excessively high operating temperature.

When the engine warms up, make sure the fans kick in; Sierra and Sapphire coolant fan wiring can melt and burn out in the fuse box. Of course, overheating could have caused any number of issues. And if an owner won't let you leave an engine idling, be very suspicious about the head gasket.

It's worth noting that the rear-wheel-drive Cosworth setup was improved for 4x4s, easily identified by twin outlets on

Coolant header tanks are prone to splitting; Sierra and RWD Sapphire parts (seen here) are rare.

the thermostat housing (compared to the RWD car's single). The cars also featured different header tanks, which are unique to Cosworths. All can crack through the plastic, but only 4x4 tanks are available new.

As for the intercooler, make sure an RS500 has its proper 'cooler, which is much bigger than the standard part (including the 4x4 version, which is larger than the RWD's). All can get clogged with oil in the pipework when turbocharger seals fail.

Exhaust [4] [3] [2] [1]

It's unusual to find a Cosworth that's not running some kind of large-bore exhaust system, probably in stainless steel. But that's okay, because OE Ford exhausts are very restrictive and gradually fall apart.

Don't be surprised if a Cosworth's exhaust is rather loud (especially under boost), but it shouldn't be blowing from any joints.

Be sure to inspect the manifold for leaks, cracks and sheared-off bolts. Bear in mind the manifolds differed from RWD to 4x4 engines, with small-turbo Escorts having unique manifolds of their own.

The turbo/exhaust downpipe may blow if securing bolts are sheared.

An original exhaust system is rare – and restrictive!

Fuel system [4] [3] [2] [1]

Poor fuelling can wipe out a Cosworth engine, leaving huge bills in its wake. And although a badly-running car may not be in immediate danger, if it's been driven for long periods the damage could already be done.

A YB that's running lean can melt its pistons under boost, while extreme overfuelling could wash oil off the cylinder bores and kill crank bearings.

Fuelling problems are often evident in misfires or poor performance. Air leaks (especially from inlet manifold gaskets) are common and awkward to trace, often causing erratic idling; a duff or dirty idle speed control valve could also be to blame.

Fuel injectors tend to be reliable, but occasionally get clogged with dirt – again leading to misfires and underfuelling. Rear-wheel-drive cars have yellow injectors as standard, while 4x4s wear blue (except for small-turbo Escorts, which have unique high-impedance parts).

Fuel pressure regulators don't tend to cause trouble unless they've been hacked around or neglected, so make sure it's all present and correct; complete with clips on the pipework and no signs of leaks. Failure can lead to major engine damage.

Small-turbo Escorts feature an airflow meter (MAF) to measure air volume; failure causes poor running, especially under light throttle.

A bad ECU chip (remap, in modern terms) can also lead to severe fuelling problems, so check that modifications are by recognised Cosworth specialists.

All YBs feature hardened valve seat inserts, which means they can run on unleaded fuel; Escorts and YBG (green-top) Sapphires are catalytic converter-equipped, too. To use unleaded, earlier cars need high-octane (97RON or above) fuel, or retarded ignition instead.

Oh, and don't forget, any RS500 should have an eight-injector fuel rail and inlet manifold, with different fuel pressure regulator and bigger throttle body. If that setup is missing, you're talking megabucks to replace it all.

RS500 fuel pressure regulator is unique to the car – and appropriately pricey.

Fuel pump

On Sierras (including Sapphires), the entire fuel pump area is prone to problems, so start with an external examination.

The pump cradle sits underneath the spare wheel well on rubber mountings, each of which can crumble and break. The cradle itself may rust away, and it's common for fuel filters to corrode, causing petrol leaks. The pump's joints and pipes can dribble, too.

Worse still, fuel pump wiring, connectors and relays can be a nightmare due to their age and exposed positions. In extreme situations a poor electrical signal reduces flow so much that the fuel injectors effectively run out of juice – which, under full boost, can melt the engine …

Fuel pumps can cause trouble – check the wiring very carefully.

Escorts are equally at risk, even though their pumps are mounted inside the petrol tank. Unlike Sierras (which have high-performance Bosch pumps), the standard Escort item is a basic Ford pump, which struggles to supply enough fuel for a mildly modified car.

With age, wear and a few tweaks, the stock pump simply isn't adequate. Add the chance of corroded connections and wiring, along with potential blockages within the fuel tank or leaks from the pump seals, and trouble is brewing. Again, low fuel pressure caused by a voltage drop means the engine will run lean on full boost – killing it spectacularly.

When buying, all you can do is check the condition of each visible component, and examine the service history to see what's been replaced; upgrades are ideal.

Wiring

Check the car's wiring loom for evidence of corrosion, overheating, chafing, splits or damaged connections. Clips and contacts can all break down, resulting in an array of faulty sensors, defective electrical components, slow starting, misfires and even engine meltdown ...

Pay particular attention to multi-plugs in the engine bay (especially underneath the nearside bonnet vent), which are exposed to damp conditions – leading to corrosion and subsequent poor running when the ECU can't communicate with engine sensors.

Many Cosworth wiring problems result from previous owners who've added alarms and immobilisers as anti-theft measures to comply with insurance stipulations. Some systems were designed to cut fuel from the pump; if you see one on a potential purchase, budget for removing the device ASAP.

Look around the car and engine bay for bodged-together or chopped-around wiring, taped-up sections, block connectors and Scotchloks. They may not be causing issues right now, but it's only a matter of time ... Besides, if an owner has skimped on something electrical, it doesn't bode well for the major mechanical components.

If the wiring is a complete mess, all is not lost. Replacement looms are available, if expensive and time-consuming to fit.

Old alarm systems were a necessary evil – beware the wiring!

Fuse box

Escort Cosworths have the same fuse box design as the regular Escort Mk5 – which means potential problems, and plenty of them!

The fuse box suffers from dry soldered joints (look for crusty deposits on the circuit board), water ingress from a leaking windscreen seal (check for dampness or green gunge), or tracks that pop up and burn out.

Fuse box trouble results in electrical failures, from minor to major. You might just find that a few bulbs don't work, but it can just as easily stop the ignition from turning the engine.

So have a good poke around, and make sure every electrical item works as it should.

Transmission

RS Cosworths feature two types of transmission – the rear-wheel-drive setup of three-door Sierras and early Sapphires, or a four-wheel-drive system on later Sapphires and all Escorts. Some Cosworths have been converted from RWD to 4x4 or vice versa, which may devalue the car.

Rear-wheel-drive Cosworths use a tough, American-sourced T5 gearbox, which can handle loads of grunt without complaint. But the T5 is notchy, even when new, and with high mileage will show signs of wear.

Most notable are tired synchromesh rings, which cause crunching when dropping down through the gears (usually from third to second) or when attempting a quick change (from third to fourth, or fourth to fifth). The only cure is a 'box rebuild.

Bear in mind there's no synchro on reverse gear, so expect to hear it crunching unless you select fifth before moving the stick.

An abused 'box may have stripped gear teeth or snapped selector forks, which you'd notice straight away! RWD cars are also prone to collapsed driveshaft bearings, which rumble while in use, eventually losing drive in one or several gears. Differentials can be dodgy,

The rear differential may be noisy; this much grime isn't a major worry.

too – sometimes whining when worn, or with a broken limited-slip differential and resultant spin from one rear wheel.

The four-wheel-drive Cosworth transmission is substantially more fragile, being based on the Sierra XR4x4 setup with MT75 gearbox. It's okay as standard, but becomes weak if the car's running high power.

Like the T5, the MT75's synchro rings fail, making crunching sounds and difficult selection in almost any gear (but usually on the downshift). A rebuild should follow. That said, the gearchange is naturally slow, so don't expect miracles. Again, there's no synchromesh on reverse.

Gearbox layshaft bearings can become noisy, especially in second or third gear. An early warning sign is rattling at idle, which sounds like an exaggerated version of a clutch bearing vibration. An MT75 on its last legs will be whining, so suspicious sounds on the test drive need careful consideration – it's only a matter of time until it loses drive altogether.

Differentials are generally hardy but will sometimes clonk, whine or feel snatchy, especially if they've been subjected to excessive torque. In such cases, the centre diff is prone to packing up, stopping drive to the front wheels – which should feel obvious on a test drive.

Knocking noises or vibrations may also be caused by broken engine mounts (especially on 4x4s) or even propshaft joints (the rubber tends to split); a loud clicking probably points to a blown CV joint. Excessively lowering a 4x4's suspension will hasten CV joint demise, so drive the car on full steering lock to listen for crunching from the bearings.

Clutch
Whether RWD or 4x4, it's essential to check a Cosworth for clutch slip – all that power and a tendency for owners to use it means clutches can have short lifespans.

Drive at around 3000rpm in fifth gear and floor the throttle to make sure road speed increases in line with engine revs. If the engine screams but the car doesn't accelerate, it'll need a new clutch.

New clutch cables are feather-light, but rapidly become stiff because the cable runs close to the exhaust downpipe (the outer sheathing melts, allowing moisture to penetrate and rust the cable).

No Cosworth clutch should be leg-breaking, though, unless it's been replaced with an uprated paddle clutch. The standard component can cope with 300bhp or more if it's not thrashed too much.

Steering

Power-assisted steering is standard on all RS Cosworths, and tends to be reliable. With age and mileage you may hear a noisy pump or see tatty gaiters, but it's unusual to find any leaks.

On the test drive, a Cosworth's steering should feel fast and precise, returning to the straight-ahead position without driver input. Wandering or vagueness should be investigated: it's fair to suspect rack wear or tired track control arm bushes, but don't rule out accident damage.

That said, when checked with the front end jacked up, it's very common to feel play in a Cosworth steering rack (Sapphires in particular), even if the rack is relatively new.

Feel for play in the steering rack, particularly on a Sapphire.

Track control bushes wear out – here they've been replaced by polyurethane.

Suspension

A standard Cosworth should handle responsively, with a firm yet compliant ride. But time and mileage takes its toll, so don't be surprised if a cheap Cosworth feels like a tired, 20-year-old motor.

Stock RWD Sapphires have a more predictable drive than early three-doors, with better road manners and less twitchiness. Four-wheel-drive Cosworths are another step ahead in terms of grip, at the cost of a little fun.

Take a test drive to feel what's going on. Wandering from the front end will likely be caused by worn track control arm bushes – a very common fault that's easily cured with polyurethane replacements. Clonking can also be due to tired bushes, but on Escorts the noise could be from the strut top cups; they're prone to cracking and creaking – a fault that's not experienced on Sierras or Sapphires.

Sloppiness at the rear (especially at speed) is probably down to worn suspension bushes; again, polyurethane should be substituted.

General vagueness could also be due to tired dampers or steering rack, while vibrations can be caused by broken engine mounts.

Check that the tyre inner edges aren't scrubbed away (probably pointing to

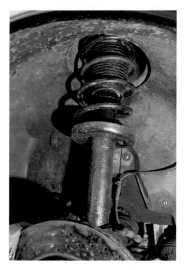

Far left: Stock front suspension should feel firm – but don't expect anything this tatty to provide a perfect ride.

Left: Rear suspension and brakes are relatively trouble-free.

worn bushes), and that the ride isn't crashy – usually the fault of dilapidated or mismatched springs or shock absorbers.

Don't be put off by sensible upgrades. Quality dampers and uprated springs can be taken for granted, but steer away from overly-lowered cars, especially 4x4s (on which driveshafts suffer if the drop's more than an inch-or-so).

Aftermarket coil-over suspension is great for track days, but might not be suitable if you're planning lots of road miles. If coil-overs are fitted, try to ensure they're good quality, because cheap kit corrodes quickly.

Brakes

Back in their day, the stopping power of rear-wheel-drive Cosworths was outstanding, boasting four-piston front callipers and large discs on the back.

But for 4x4s the story wasn't so good: while the rear discs were now vented, mainstream floating callipers were used up front. Even when new, they feel poor compared to modern performance machines.

A test drive is the best way to establish whether they're working properly. The pedal should feel firm yet communicative, and pressing it should stop the car efficiently (even from high speed) without veering to one side.

Front brakes are prone to juddering; callipers may be sticky.

The most likely fault you'll find is juddering through the steering wheel and pedal, even with relatively low pressure; it's sometimes accompanied by a clicking noise from the pads. The usual cause is warped or contaminated front discs, especially if they've been used hard or overheated on track. All Cosworths consume discs and pads pretty regularly – it's simply a by-product of the performance on offer.

Judder may have a more sinister cause (a front suspension component, for example), but a simple case of worn pads may be to blame for squealing or grating sounds.

Heavy vibrations from the brakes or pulling to one side may be due to sticking front callipers, especially on the superior RWD four-pot setup – if so, you'll be able to feel the heat by placing your hand near (not on) the front wheel after a short drive; the disc on that side may also be excessively scored.

Cosworth rear callipers can seize in the on or off position; it's easy to tell if it's dragging by jacking up the rear end and ensuring the wheels spin freely. If it's stuck

Cosworth 4x4s wear vented rear discs; callipers seize on or off.

off, it won't work when you operate the brake pedal and/or handbrake lever.

As with any secondhand car, be sure to check the braking system everywhere for leaks and corrosion – leaving a Cosworth unused will not only cause the discs to rust but also reduce the effectiveness of the pads.

Uprated brakes are common, and ideal if they're decent-quality and functioning correctly. Be aware, though, that race callipers usually lack weather seals needed for winter road use, and if you're trying before you buy, don't forget a short test drive won't give track pads time to warm up properly.

ABS

Cosworths have a decent ABS (anti-lock braking) system as standard. The ABS shouldn't interfere when driving (if it cuts in early there's a problem) and, of course, the dashboard warning lamp shouldn't be aglow after the ignition start-up sequence.

ABS pumps occasionally fail (Sapphires are more prone than other models) but the most likely culprit for an annoying ABS light is a dirty or damaged wheel sensor, which is cheap and easy to replace.

Faulty ABS may also be caused by defective wiring, a fuse issue, or even the fluid level sender. Tracing problems can be slow and costly, so be careful if there's no servo assistance (an exceptionally heavy pedal) or no ABS at all (when the wheels lock up and skid under heavy braking).

Wheels and tyres

Wide alloy wheels were fitted to Cosworths as standard; Sierras of all descriptions left the factory with 7x15in rims and 205/50ZR15 tyres, while Escorts wore 8x16in alloys and 225/45/16ZR rubber.

The wheels are pretty tough, but misshapen rims cause vibrations, and bent or heavily-kerbed alloys could be expensive to repair. Three-doors and RS500s have diamond-cut wheel faces, on which the factory lacquer is prone to peeling off; it's a professional job to restore.

Check the tyres for condition and wear, paying attention to unusual scrubbing that suggests dodgy geometry – maybe from a faulty suspension component, but possibly due to accident damage.

Budget-brand tyres suggest servicing has been skimped on, so view them as a warning sign of the owner's commitment to maintenance.

Lacquer lifts from three-door diamond-cut alloy wheels.

Inner wings

Cosworth inner wings are basically standard Sierra spec, albeit with minor alterations depending on model. The only real identification feature is found on three-doors, which have an inverted keyhole-shaped cutout in the bulkhead behind the brake servo, as opposed to the standard Sierra's single round hole (all Cosworths have ABS, but it wasn't available on the three-door Sierra 1.3 or 1.6), plus four mounting

bolts rather than two. Sapphire Cosworths also have this bulkhead, but as various other specs were ABS-equipped, it doesn't tell us very much.

Similarly, four-wheel drive machines have semi-circular cutouts on the front chassis rails to make room for the driveshafts – but non-Cosworth 4x4 Sapphires were built by Ford with the same shell.

Needless to say, Cosworth inner wings rust as badly as mundane models. Check the strut towers for rot, especially at the nearside underneath the header tank. Serious cases see the turrets collapse.

Inverted keyhole shape is pressed into a proper Cosworth's bulkhead; this home-cut example is on a non-genuine shell.

Look carefully for rot where the inner wings meet the bulkhead.

That's not a good sign – rot around the front suspension turret.

An Escort Cosworth battery tray –
lacking the traditional rot, surprisingly.

Good bulkhead insulator pads are
extremely rare.

Examine the inner wings where they meet the bulkhead beneath the bonnet hinges. Sierras and Sapphires suffer from stress fractures, which crack the paint, allowing moisture ingress and subsequent corrosion. Major rust can be serious, making the car banana-shaped (exhibited in a closing-up of the exterior panel gap between front wings and doors).

A particular problem with Escorts is the battery tray, which can rot away; Sierras allow rainwater to drain, but on Escorts it sits in the tray, doing its worst …

Naturally, you'll need to inspect the inner wings for creases, suspicious paintwork and other rust, which can be telltales of accident damage. Ensure the slam panel and wings have a neat bead of seam sealer where they join – if not, they've been replaced. Make sure the slam panel is wearing its factory VIN tag and body colour plate, too.

If you're investing in a standard three-door, check the bulkhead insulator pad – good replacements are unavailable anywhere. Similarly, Escort underbonnet sound deadening drops to bits, and their plastic turbo heat shields are much in demand.

Front wings

Front wings rust around the wheelarches and rear edges where they meet the sills. Check they have a neat line of seam sealer where they join the bonnet slam panel – they may have been replaced because of rust, but accident damage is equally likely …

Genuine three-door wings were pre-stamped with square holes around the wheelarches (bunged with plastic screw clips), although they're impossible to see with the arch extensions in place.

Three-doors often have the metal of their

Right: Factory seam sealer looks neat and tidy …

Far right: … but seam sealer on replacement front wings isn't quite as smart.

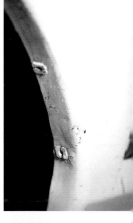

wheelarches trimmed back behind the extensions to accept aftermarket wheels – be aware that it can have a detrimental effect on value.

Stand back and inspect the panel gaps between the front wings and doors to ensure they're not closer at the top than the bottom – a sign of a rusty and/or abused Sierra or Sapphire that's folded up where the bulkhead meets the inner wings.

Oh, and remember that although Sierra/Sapphire wings are the same as basic models, Escort parts are unique to the Cosworth – thus more expensive and unavailable new.

Genuine three-door Cosworth bodyshells have plastic clips factory-pressed into their wheelarches.

Grille

Three-door grilles are prone to snapped fixing lugs at the corners above the headlamps. Needless to say, they're pricey parts to replace.

Sapphire lugs also snap, but the grille isn't expensive to source.

Front grille mounting clips can snap – shown here on an RS500.

Front bumper

Front bumpers are susceptible to breakage and countless stone chips. The front splitter (the black lower spoiler) is vulnerable to being ripped off on road humps, especially on Escorts (which also have damage-prone hockey sticks on each corner), so don't be surprised if it's tatty or missing altogether.

Sapphire front bumpers

A genuine Cosworth towing eye is straight.

The normal Sierra towing eye is this twisted shape.

have a tendency to flap around at the sides when their mounting brackets break. They also sag across the bottom, but are still plentiful secondhand – which is the complete opposite of the RS500 front bumper, which is slightly different from the standard three-door part and carries an extremely hefty price tag (if you can find one).

Oh, and check the towing eye poking through the bumper is the proper Cosworth straight loop rather than a twisted shape found on ordinary Sierras and Sapphires. Towing eye covers go missing too, but are easy to replace.

Bonnet

Only rear-wheel-drive Sapphires use a stock bonnet – all other Cosworths have factory-pressed cutouts for vents. Paintwork above the turbocharger on RWD bonnets goes crazy, but vented versions are almost as bad. Don't be surprised to see a 4x4 vented bonnet on a RWD Sapphire – it's a useful upgrade.

All are prone to stone chips, so it's fair to expect non-original paint. Left untreated – or if the car's been neglected – bonnets may also rust, especially along the leading edge.

Vented bonnets were factory pressed. It's common to find cracked paint above the turbo.

Floorpan and chassis   4️⃣ 3️⃣ 2️⃣ 1️⃣

Most of the Cosworth floorpan is stock Sierra (yes, even the Escort), albeit featuring an enlarged transmission tunnel to fit the bigger gearbox (it's notably wider near the clutch pedal).

Of course, the underside rots like a Sierra too, so search for corrosion (holes, splits, filler or fresh paint/underseal) and/or evidence of accident damage (creases or ripples).

Pay particular attention to the front chassis rails and crossmember. It's not unusual to find crushed box sections or dented floors caused by careless jacking.

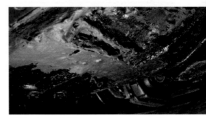

What could heavy underseal be hiding? In this case, maybe an untidy floorpan?

Most importantly, check the rear chassis box sections, which can corrode very badly near the spring seats. Rot here is tricky and pricey to put right.

Rear chassis rails are a prime rot-spot; check around the springs in particular.

Sills   4️⃣ 3️⃣ 2️⃣ 1️⃣

Inner and outer sills rot away, usually from the back working forwards. Sierras and Sapphires are bad, but Escorts are worse – otherwise-mint-looking Cosworths can be hiding serious

Jacking point covers often go astray.

Below: Inner and outer sills may corrode; these have been replaced, sadly, removing the chassis number in the process.

corrosion behind the side skirts. The problem starts when moisture sits between skirt and sill; a preventative measure is to drill drain holes out of sight underneath.

Ensure the skirt's jacking point covers are all intact; they often go astray (especially from Sapphires), and can be costly to replace.

Similarly, Escort skirt fixing clips break when removed, and are unavailable new.

Roof

Every Sierra Cosworth, Sapphire Cosworth and RS500 has a sunroof, as do the majority of Escorts – only standard (non-Luxury-spec) Escorts and genuine Sierra or Escort Motorsport shells (or replicas built around base models ...) do not.

It's rare to see rust bubbling around the roof, but the sunroof's metal framework can rot; some owners don't realise until the whole glass panel pops out at speed.

Any sunroof may seize, so ensure it still works. If you can, try to make sure it doesn't leak, which is a distinct possibility.

Electric sunroofs were optional on late-spec Sapphires and Escorts. If fitted, test the motor operates in all directions.

Doors

Like most Fords, Cosworths' door bottoms rust away, with rot spreading from the edges, up the skins and around the windows. They're the same as standard-model doors, though, so aren't especially rare.

The rubbing strips along each side of the car are a different matter. They ripple when removed incorrectly (eg for paintwork repairs), and three-door parts in particular fetch big money.

Rubbing strips ripple when removed; they're tricky to find new.

Corrosion occurs around doors and window frames.

Rear wings

Rusty rear wheelarches will be pretty obvious, and can be found on any model. Muck and moisture trapped behind them will bubble away through the inner arches, rear wings and into the cabin.

Escorts in particular corrode around the fuel filler aperture. Later cars are less prone – they have a flap, whereas earlier models feature a flush locking cap.

You won't be able to see them unless the plastic extensions are removed, but note that three-door Sierra rear wheelarches are factory-stamped with square holes to accept plastic clips.

Three-doors may also rust around the rear side windows – a big job to put right.

If you're buying an RS500, make sure it has

Rear wheelarch rot on a Sapphire will eat away the entire door shut.

an electric aerial in the rear wing, just above the filler cap – it's standard-fit, and should retract when the tailgate is unlocked.

Windows ④ ③ ② ①

Check all the glass matches – especially where a VIN or registration number has been etched in. Don't forget Cosworths are still desirable to thieves …

Make sure the windscreen is undamaged – heated 'screens are expensive to replace, and were standard on Sapphires and Luxury-model Escorts.

This Sapphire's heated front windscreen cracked when the car was jacked incorrectly.

Rust bubbling away beneath windscreen rubber.

Bodyshells are pretty weak, and it's possible to crack the windscreen just from jacking in the wrong place – so beware!

Take a look at the window seals on any Sierra/Sapphire – they corrode and blister, and kink if not removed properly. Good replacements for three-doors are very pricey.

Check for rust around the bonded windscreens, too – probably caused by careless aftermarket fitting.

Lights ④ ③ ② ①

Most lights are shared with lesser models, but genuine three-door and Escort front indictor lenses are unavailable new. Demand is now for orange indicators, which over the years have often been swapped for clear.

Three-door headlight lenses go yellow with age, and are again unavailable new from Ford; Sierra Ghia parts are the same, so may be found secondhand.

Only 4x4 Sapphires had smoked rear lights from new, but they were often retrofitted to earlier cars.

Sapphire 4x4 wears smoked rear light clusters.

Boot lid ④ ③ ② ①

Examine around the edge of any boot lid for rust, as well as spoiler mounting points. Escort tailgates and Sapphire boot lids in particular are prone to rotting; they're mere standard Ford panels from lesser models, but difficult to find in good condition.

Tailgates and boot lids crumble around the edge.

Rear spoiler ④ ③ ② ①

Make sure the rear spoiler is firmly attached, without rot around its mountings. Check paintwork for cracks. Be dubious of a whale-tail without Ford stamps.

Remember the large, upper rear wing was a delete option on later Escorts, so don't be suspicious if it's absent. Likewise, don't assume there's anything wrong with a Sapphire if the rear spoiler is fully colour-coded – the very last cars left the factory like that.

Pay special attention to the rear spoiler on an RS500. Unlike the regular three-

door, there's an extra lip on the upper wing and a lower spoiler too; if the central cutout for the whale-tail support appears to be an afterthought (not part of the moulding), it's a 20iS spoiler rather than genuine RS500.

Rear bumper

Stand back and look at the car's rear bumper – dodgy gaps or poor alignment may highlight accident damage. Sapphires are prone to wonky bumpers, caused when their mounting brackets corrode and snap. It's almost impossible to find one new.

Sagging Sapphire rear bumpers are common – as are accident-damaged nearside rear wings.

Escort bumpers often melt around the exhaust tailpipe. Some have been hacked around to accept a larger-bore pipe – it's up to you to decide what's acceptable.

Seats

Recaro front seats and matching rear bench are Cosworth-specific. Which, of course, means they're rare and expensive if you need to replace them.

All three-door models (including RS500s) have grey cloth upholstery; a similar material is found on many Sapphires. Standard-fit trim in Escorts is grey cloth with Hexagon pattern. All are durable, if susceptible to staining, sagging and wearing through on the driver's side bolster. Be wary of tears and cigarette burns, because the cloth is hard to repair.

Cosworth leather looks classy, but cracks heavily with age and wear.

Driver's seat bolsters wear through, whether leather or cloth.

Dark grey leather was optional from 1989, and often seen in Sapphires and Luxury-spec Escorts. Again, it's prone to deteriorating on the driver's side bolster, along with generalised cracking. Look out for rips, scuffs and tatty stitching, too.

Seat frames are durable, but can eventually collapse underneath. The foam bases tend to break down, as does the padding within those side bolsters.

Luxury-spec Escorts were available with heated seats as an optional extra; check to ensure they work.

Door cards

It's not unknown for owners to buy complete interiors simply to source good door cards, such is their rarity.

Three-door models in particular are a problem, with vinyl trim going wrinkly on the armrests.

Door card material peels away from the backing – here in a leather-clad Sapphire cabin.

Sapphire cards are renowned for shrinking and lifting away where they meet the glass, which can be expensive to repair.

Ensure all door cards aren't torn, and make sure they match the seats – especially if the car you're buying has leather trim.

Dashboard 4 3 2 1

Most of the Cosworth's interior is uninspiring Ford plastic, but at least it's durable – except for Sierra and Sapphire dashboard tops that, although identical to run-of-the-mill models, are becoming impossible to replace. Small splits can be repaired, but major cracks mean a whole new dash.

Pay attention to the dashboard top where it meets the windscreen, and especially around the speaker grille on three-door cars, for which a mint replacement can cost four figures!

Look out for cracks in the dashboard top.

Instruments 4 3 2 1

Cosworth dials don't generally go wrong, but they are specific to each model. Sierra and Sapphire milometers flip back to zero after 99,999, and are easy to adjust – so don't trust the mileage to be genuine unless it's backed up by paperwork.

It's common to find aftermarket auxiliary gauges, often mounted in place of dashboard heater vents or on the driver's A-pillar. If they're wired in neatly it's a bonus, but if they're chopped into the dashboard it's a big negative.

Cosworth clocks are remarkably easy to wind back ...

Escorts feature white dials, with faces that go blotchy over time. They also have a digital clock set into the dashboard – it's the same part found in some other Escorts, and equally prone to disappearing digits.

Finally, make sure everything on the dashboard graphic display lights up correctly to tell you when a door is open or a bulb is out.

Switchgear 4 3 2 1

Stalks and switches are the same as found on normal Sierras and Escorts, so shouldn't be tricky to replace when broken.

Don't forget that dodgy electrics (especially on an Escort) can mean a broken fuse box, so make sure all the bulbs, fans and lights work properly.

Aftermarket auxiliary gauges may provide handy pointers to the engine's health.

Heater motors sometimes pack up (completely, or on a couple of speeds), but be more concerned if the car has air-conditioning (it was optional on late Sapphires and Luxury-spec Escorts) that refuses to crank up or turn cold.

Headlining 4 3 2 1

Check the headlining of Sapphires in particular, which may be sagging, especially towards the rear of the car. Look out for stains, notably around the sunroof if the seals are leaking.

Rear parcel shelf 4 3 2 1

Again a standard Ford part, but the rear parcel shelf in any three-door is rare, costly and usually found in poor condition – check it's not especially bowed or had holes chopped in for aftermarket speakers.

Centre console 4 3 2 1

Centre consoles can be tatty and a poor fit. In an Escort, ensure the gearlever gaiter is in good condition – they don't wear well, and are available only as part of the complete centre console.

Steering wheel 4 3 2 1

Steering wheels tend to be tough, although the stitching may come loose from the leather rim. Aftermarket upgrades are common.

Original Cosworth steering wheels tend to be tough.

Small-turbo Escorts include an airbag.
Make sure the dashboard warning light works when you turn on the ignition.

Electrical motors 4 3 2 1

Don't forget to make sure all those electrical gadgets are present and correct.

Electric windows and central locking motors get sticky, electric mirrors stop working and sunroof motors (a rare optional extra) can pack up. Heated windscreens can be dodgy too, but are hard to test unless it's a cold day or the windows are misted.

Always be conscious of a wiring or fuse box problem being to blame for electrical malfunctions, with associated repair difficulties.

Luggage compartment 4 3 2 1

Hundreds of Cosworths – especially RWD versions – have exited the highway in a backwards direction, so it's not unusual to see signs of accident damage in the luggage compartment.

Lift the boot carpet to inspect the spare wheel well and floor for splits, rust or creases; you don't want to see filler, underseal or fresh paint either – Ford's factory finish wasn't glossy, so if it's shiny it's been resprayed.

Similarly, examine the rear inner wings to look for welds and creases, which will show if the rear quarters have been replaced or straightened out.

Rear light seals and rubbers around the boot lid can deteriorate too, letting in rainwater. In turn this leads to rust, so feel all around the luggage compartment mat for signs of dampness from leaks.

A good, clean boot floor means this car isn't hiding any secrets.

Evaluation procedure

Add up the total points.
168 = excellent (possibly concours); 126 = good; 84 = average; 42 = poor.
Cars scoring over 118 should be completely useable.
Cars scoring between 87 and 117 will need very careful assessment.
Cars scoring between 42 and 86 may require full restoration.

10 Auctions
– sold! Another way to buy your dream

Auction pros & cons

Pros: Prices will usually be lower than those of dealers or private sellers and you might grab a real bargain on the day. Auctioneers have usually established clear title with the seller. At the venue you can often examine documentation relating to the vehicle.

Cons: You have to rely on a sketchy catalogue description of condition and history. The opportunity to inspect is limited and you cannot drive the car. Auction cars are often a little below par and may require some work. It's easy to overbid. There will usually be a buyer's premium to pay in addition to the auction hammer price.

Which auction?

Auctions by established auctioneers are advertised in car magazines and on the auction houses' websites. A catalogue or a simple printed list of the lots for auctions might only be available a day or two ahead, though often lots are listed and pictured on auctioneers' websites much earlier. Contact the auction company to ask if previous auction selling prices are available, as this is useful information (details of past sales are often displayed on websites).

Catalogue, entry fee and payment details

When you purchase the catalogue of the vehicles in the auction, it often acts as a ticket allowing two people to attend the viewing days and the auction. Catalogue details tend to be comparatively brief, but will include information such as 'one owner from new, low mileage, full service history,' etc. It will also usually show a guide price to give you some idea of what to expect to pay, and state what is charged as a 'buyer's premium.' The catalogue will also contain details of acceptable forms of payment. At the fall of the hammer an immediate deposit is usually required, the balance payable within 24 hours. If the plan is to pay by cash there may be a cash limit. Some auctions will accept payment by debit card. Sometimes credit or charge cards are acceptable, but will often incur an extra charge. A bank draft or bank transfer will have to be arranged in advance with your own bank as well as with the auction house. No car will be released before all payments are cleared. If delays occur in payment transfers then storage costs can accrue.

Buyer's premium

A buyer's premium will be added to the hammer price: don't forget this in your calculations. It is not usual for there to be a further state tax or local tax on the purchase price and/or on the buyer's premium.

Viewing

In some instances it's possible to view on the day, or days before, as well as in the hours prior to, the auction. Occasionally there are auction officials available who are willing to help out by opening engine and luggage compartments and to allow you to inspect the interior. While the officials may start the engine for you, a test drive is out of the question. Crawling under and around the car as much as you want is permitted, but you can't suggest that the car you are interested in be jacked up, or attempt to do the job yourself. You can also ask to see any documentation available.

Bidding

Before you take part in the auction, decide your maximum bid – and stick to it! It may take a while for the auctioneer to reach the lot you are interested in, so use that time to observe how other bidders behave. When it's the turn of your car, attract the auctioneer's attention and make an early bid – but not too early, or you'll risk inflating price. The auctioneer will then look to you for a reaction every time another bid is made. Usually the bids will be in fixed increments until the bidding slows, when smaller increments will often be accepted before the hammer falls. If you want to withdraw from the bidding, make sure the auctioneer understands your intentions – a vigorous shake of the head when he or she looks to you for the next bid should do the trick!

Assuming you are the successful bidder, the auctioneer will note your card or paddle number, and from that moment on you will be responsible for the vehicle.

If the car is unsold, either because it failed to reach the reserve or because there was little interest, it may be possible to negotiate with the owner, via the auctioneers, after the sale is over.

Successful bid

There are two more items to think about: how to get the car home, and insurance. If you can't drive the car, your own or a hired trailer is one way; another is to have the vehicle shipped using the facilities of a local company. The auction house will also have details of companies specialising in the transfer of cars.

Insurance for immediate cover can usually be purchased on site, but it may be more cost-effective to make arrangements with your own insurance company in advance, and then call to confirm the full details.

eBay and other online auctions

eBay and other online auctions could land you a car at a bargain price, though you'd be foolhardy to bid without examining the car first – something most vendors encourage. A useful feature of eBay is that the geographical location of the car is shown, so you can narrow your choices to those within a realistic radius of home. Be prepared to be outbid in the last few moments of the auction. Remember, your bid is binding and that it will be very, very difficult to get restitution in the case of a crooked vendor fleecing you – caveat emptor!

Be aware that some cars offered for sale in online auctions are 'ghost' cars. Don't part with any cash without being sure that the vehicle does actually exist and is as described (usually pre-bidding inspection is possible).

Auctioneers

Barrett-Jackson www.barrett-jackson.com **Barons** www.barons-auctions.com **Bonhams** www.bonhams.com **British Car Auctions (BCA)** www.bca-europe.com or www.british-car-auctions.co.uk **Cheffins** www.cheffins.co.uk **Christies** www.christies.com **Coys** www.coys.co.uk **eBay** www.eBay.com **H&H** www.classic-auctions.co.uk **RM** www.rmauctions.com **Shannons** www.shannons.com.au **Silver** www.silverauctions.com

11 Paperwork
– correct documentation is essential!

A well-cared-for Cosworth will often come complete with a comprehensive pile of paperwork.

The paper trail

Classic, collector and prestige cars usually come with a large portfolio of paperwork accumulated and passed on by a succession of proud owners. This documentation represents the real history of the car and from it can be deduced the level of care the car has received, how much it's been used, which specialists have worked on it and the dates of major repairs and restorations. All of this information will be priceless to you as the new owner, so be very wary of cars with little paperwork to support their claimed history.

Registration documents

All countries/states have some form of registration for private vehicles, whether it's like the American 'pink slip' system or the British 'log book' system.

It is essential to check that the registration document is genuine, that it relates to the car in question, and that all the vehicle's details are correctly recorded, including chassis/VIN and engine numbers (if these are shown). If you are buying from the previous owner, his or her name and address will be recorded in the document: this will not be the case if you are buying from a dealer.

In the UK the current (Euro-aligned) registration document is named V5C, and is printed in coloured sections of blue, green and pink. The blue section relates to the car specification, the green section has details of the new owner, and the pink section is sent to the DVLA in the UK when the car is sold. A small section in yellow deals with selling the car within the motor trade.

In the UK the DVLA will provide details of earlier keepers of the vehicle upon payment of a small fee, and much can be learned in this way.

If the car has a foreign registration there may be expensive and time-consuming formalities to complete. Do you really want the hassle?

Roadworthiness certificate

Most country/state administrations require that vehicles are regularly tested to prove that they are safe to use on the public highway and do not produce excessive emissions. In the UK that test (the 'MoT') is carried out at approved testing stations, for a fee. In the USA the requirement varies, but most states insist on an emissions test every two years as a minimum, while the police are charged with pulling over unsafe-looking vehicles.

In the UK the test is required on an annual basis once a vehicle becomes three years old. Of particular relevance for older cars is that the certificate issued includes the mileage reading recorded at the test date and, therefore, becomes an independent record of that car's history. Ask the seller if previous certificates are available. Without an MoT the vehicle should be trailered to its new home, unless you insist that a valid MoT is part of the deal (not such a bad idea this, as at least you will know the car was roadworthy on the day it was tested and you don't need to wait for the old certificate to expire before having the test done).

Road licence

The administration of every country/state charges some kind of tax for the use of its road system, the actual form of the 'road licence' and, how it is displayed, varying enormously country to country and state to state.

Whatever the form of the 'road licence,' it must relate to the vehicle carrying it and must be present and valid if the car is to be driven on the public highway legally. The value of the licence will depend on the length of time it will continue to be valid.

In the UK if a car is untaxed because it has not been used for a period of time, the owner has to inform the licensing authorities, otherwise the vehicle's date-related registration number will be lost and there will be a painful amount of paperwork to get it re-registered.

Certificates of authenticity

For many makes of collectible car it is possible to get a certificate proving the age and authenticity, but it's unlikely you'll find anything of the kind to accompany a relatively modern Ford. If you want to obtain more details of a car's history, the relevant owners' club is the best starting point – all models of Cosworth have club registrars, who may already have details on file about your potential purchase.

Valuation certificate

Hopefully, the vendor will have a recent valuation certificate, or letter signed by a recognised expert stating how much he, or she, believes the particular car to be worth (such documents, together with photos, are usually needed to get 'agreed value' insurance). Generally, such documents should act only as confirmation of your own assessment of the car rather than a guarantee of value. The easiest way to find out how to obtain a formal valuation is to contact the relevant owners' club, who will usually need to see an RS in the metal before issuing a valuation.

Service history

Although many RS Cosworths are maintained by specialists, plenty have been serviced at home by enthusiastic (and hopefully capable) owners for a good number of years. Nevertheless, try to obtain as much service history and other paperwork pertaining to the car as you can. Naturally, dealer stamps or specialist garage receipts score most points in the value stakes. However, anything helps in the great authenticity game – items like the original bill of sale, handbook, parts invoices and repair bills add to the story and the character of the car. Even a brochure correct to the year of the car's manufacture is a useful document and something that you could well have to search hard to locate in future years. If the seller claims that the car has been restored, then expect receipts and other evidence from a specialist restorer.

If the seller claims to have carried out regular servicing, ask what work was completed, when, and seek some evidence of it being carried out. Your assessment of the car's overall condition should tell you whether the seller's claims are genuine.

Restoration photographs

If the seller tells you that the car has been restored, expect to be shown a series of photographs taken while the restoration was under way. Pictures at various stages, and from various angles, should help you gauge the thoroughness of the work. If you buy the car, ask if you can have all the photographs, as they form an important part of the vehicle's history. It's surprising how many sellers are happy to part with their car and accept your cash, but want to hang on to their photographs. If that's the case, you may be able to persuade the vendor to get a set of copies made.

12 What's it worth?
– let your head rule your heart

Condition
If the car you've been looking at is really bad, you've probably not bothered to use the marking system in chapter 9 – 60 minute evaluation. You may not have even got as far as using that chapter at all!

If you did use the marking system in chapter 9, you'll know whether the car is in Excellent (maybe Concours), Good, Average or Poor condition or, perhaps, somewhere in between.

Many classic car magazines run a regular price guide. If you haven't bought the latest editions, do so now and compare their suggested values for the

Well-engineered modifications may command a premium when properly done.

model you are thinking of buying: also look at the auction prices they're reporting.

Values have been increasing slowly, but some models will always be more sought-after than others. Trends can change, too. The values published in the magazines tend to vary from one magazine to another, as do their scales of condition, so read carefully the guidance notes they provide. Of course, a truly outstanding example or a recent show winner could be worth more than the highest scale published. Bear in mind, too, that magazine estimates for humble Fords can be rather low.

Assuming that the car you have in mind is not in concours condition, then relate the level of condition that you judge the car to be in with the appropriate guide price. How does the figure compare with the asking price? Before you start haggling with the seller, consider what effect any variation from standard specification might have on the car's value.

If you're buying from a dealer, remember there will be a dealer's premium on the price.

Desirable options/extras
Before deciding what a Cosworth is worth to you, work out what you

Mint, factory-original parts tend to fetch more cash than aftermarket additions.

really want from the car. If your heart is set on an Imperial Blue Escort, a white three-door probably won't fit the bill – regardless of how nice it might be.

And if you're thinking of a Cosworth to use everyday, a good, clean Sapphire will make more sense than a concours RS500 – it's much better to leave that as an investment that's only brought out in summer.

Likewise, your plans for the car have maximum influence on its value to you as a whole. There's no point buying a highly-tuned, 500bhp Cosworth if what you really want is a factory-original showpiece. If you enjoy track days, a ready-modified machine makes more financial sense than starting from scratch; while you're there, will you decide you prefer the raw excitement of a rear-wheel-drive to the grip of a 4x4? Many cars have been converted from one setup to the other, which involves massive outlay that's worthless to some potential buyers.

As such, it's wisest to first decide on your ideal type of Cosworth (Sierra, Sapphire or Escort), followed by its condition and specification. Any extras may then be seen as a bonus – with, potentially, adjustment in asking price for bad points.

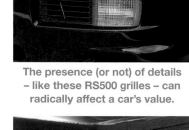

The presence (or not) of details – like these RS500 grilles – can radically affect a car's value.

Nevertheless, certain specifications and originality levels usually attract more buyers, reflected by a correspondingly higher value:
• Factory-original specification – correct parts for the model and year, even including tyre type.
• Matching numbers – including the chassis plates, inner sills and engine numbers (except RS500s). It's also desirable if date stamps on components (eg wheels and windows) correspond with the age of the car.
• Colour – some classic shades are more desirable due to appearance or rarity. For example, Moonstone Blue is the rarest and (arguably) prettiest paintwork for an RS500.
• Well-engineered modifications, preferably

Don't be put off by a large-bore stainless exhaust system – most Cossies have them.

backed up by receipts from a recognised Cosworth specialist.
• Escort Monte Carlo limited edition.
• Leather interior, electric sunroof and air-conditioning may command a slight premium on Sapphires and Luxury-model Escorts.

Undesirable features
Few factory specifications will render a Cosworth undesirable, although some of the more restrained paint schemes have less appeal to buyers.

Some owner-made alterations, though, may have a detrimental effect:
• Suspicious identity – mismatched history, missing identity numbers or odd-looking shell can have a very negative impact on value.
• Incorrect specification – especially on RS500s, but relevant to any show-condition Cosworth. The wrong parts mean money may be deducted.
• Cosmetic alterations, including non-standard spoilers, bodykit, generic alloy wheels, colour change or interior customisation (but upgraded parts from higher-spec Cosworths, such as RS500 front bumper, may add value).
• Bad tuning or poorly-executed modifications – half-hearted engine upgrades could be about to go bang.

Striking a deal
Negotiate on the basis of your condition assessment, mileage, and fault rectification cost. Also take into account the car's specification. Be realistic about the value, but don't be completely intractable: a small compromise on the part of the vendor or buyer will often facilitate a deal at little real cost.

13 Do you really want to restore?
– it'll take longer and cost more than you think

You could just about rescue a genuine three-door from this state of dereliction, but your pockets wouldn't like it.

Do you really want to restore this car? Yes? Without the RS Cosworth tag, your answer may be very different.

Cosworths corrode and crumble like any other Ford of the period, rotting beneath the surface while maintaining a glossy outward appearance. The difference is, with a Cosworth you've the added worries of highly-stressed mechanicals, years of hard, fast abuse, plus countless unique-to-Cosworth components and ultra-pricey parts. Oh yes, and a relatively large sum to pay for it all in the first place.

On the flipside, of course, the Cosworth's humble origins make it a pretty easy car to work on. Most jobs are within reach of a decent DIY mechanic, and even the prized YB powerplant is straightforward enough for a home spannerman who's adept at engine rebuilds. That said, anyone aiming at creating a big-bhp unit would be advised to consult a specialist, unless they have plenty of experience – if only because the consequences of a poorly-tuned Cosworth can severely damage your wallet.

Cosworth bodywork is a different story. Almost everything that rusts is standard Ford fare (inner wings, chassis rails and sills require the same amounts of welding whether it's a Cossie or a 1.3L), but anything that's Cosworth-specific (including vented bonnets, spoilers and half the Escort's outer panels) will be expensive and hard to source.

As for those ultra-rare items – such as RS500 front bumpers – you really need to explore the cost of obtaining replacements for broken or missing parts and factor them into the purchase price of a particular car. Similarly, interior trim is available, at a price (try finding a mint, uncracked three-door dashboard and see how you get on).

In the majority of cases, it's easiest and cheapest to buy a good or excellent car that can be tweaked to your standards over the course of ownership, allowing you to enjoy it in the meantime.

But the cost of bringing a tidy Cosworth up to concours condition can easily double your initial outlay. A partly-restored car could be hiding innumerable problems, from filled bodywork to a decrepit engine, and once your project is under way it's very tempting to renew parts you previously thought were acceptable.

So if you demand the absolute best and don't want to buy a perfect showpiece, you might as well start with a total basket case. Tackling a nut-and-bolt stripdown to the standards demanded by Cosworth enthusiasts won't be cheap or easy, but it's worthwhile to ensure a terrific result that also includes any personal touches you may fancy.

Talking of which, another question should be, do you really want to modify this car? Tuning, for many, is an integral part of Cosworth ownership, and if you're using the car regularly you'll probably want to increase its engine's power. Buying a ready-built car is invariably the most cost-effective option, but poor setup and home-brewed mods may bite you in the pocket – so tread very carefully.

Sorting out someone else's work from a pile of parts could present a serious headache.

14 Paint problems
– bad complexion, including dimples, pimples and bubbles

Paint faults generally occur due lack of protection/maintenance, or to poor preparation prior to a respray or touch-up. Some of the following conditions may be present in the car you're looking at.

Orange peel
This appears as an uneven paint surface, similar to the appearance of the skin of an orange. The fault is caused by the failure of atomized paint droplets to flow into each other when they hit the surface. It's sometimes possible to rub out the effect with proprietary paint cutting/rubbing compound or very fine grades of abrasive paper. A respray may be necessary in severe cases. Remember, though, that Ford's factory finish often had an orange peel effect, and the paintwork could be original.

Cracking
Severe cases are likely to have been caused by too heavy an application of paint (or filler beneath the paint). Also, insufficient stirring of the paint before application can lead to the components being improperly mixed, and cracking can result.

Incompatibility with the paint already on the panel can have a similar effect. To rectify the problem it is necessary to rub down to a smooth, sound finish before respraying the problem area.

Crazing
Sometimes the paint takes on a crazed rather than a cracked appearance when the problems mentioned under 'Cracking' are present. This problem can also be caused by a reaction between the underlying surface and the paint. Paint removal and respraying the problem area is usually the only solution.

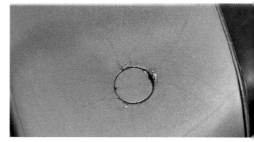

Paint on Cosworth rear spoilers cracks and crazes, especially around mounting holes.

Blistering
Almost always caused by corrosion of the metal beneath the paint. Usually perforation will be found in the metal, and the damage will usually be worse than that suggested by the area of blistering. The metal will have to be repaired before repainting.

Micro blistering
Usually the result of an economy respray, where inadequate heating has allowed moisture to settle on the car before

Rust bubbling up around an Escort Cosworth's rear wheelarch.

Micro blistering on a Sapphire's resprayed rear wing.

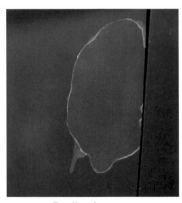

Peeling lacquer.

spraying. Consult a paint specialist, but usually damaged paint will have to be removed before partial or full respraying. Can also be caused by car covers that don't 'breathe.'

Fading
Some colours, especially reds, are prone to fading if subjected to strong sunlight for long periods without the benefit of polish protection. Sometimes proprietary paint restorers and/or paint cutting/rubbing compounds will retrieve the situation. Often a respray is the only real solution.

Peeling
Often a problem with metallic paintwork when the sealing laquer becomes damaged and begins to peel off. Poorly applied paint may also peel. The remedy is to strip and start again!

Dimples
Dimples in the paintwork are caused by the residue of polish (particularly silicone types) not being removed properly before respraying. Paint removal and repainting is the only solution.

Dents
Small dents are usually easily cured by the 'Dentmaster' or equivalent process, which sucks or pushes out the dent (as long as the paint surface is still intact). Companies offering dent removal services usually come to your home: consult your telephone directory.

15 Problems due to lack of use
– just like their owners, Cosworths need exercise!

Letting the grass grow around a Cosworth probably means it'll need some recommissioning before use.

Cars, like humans, are at their most efficient if they exercise regularly. A run of at least ten miles, once a week, is recommended for any RS Cosworth.

Seized components
• Pistons in callipers, slave and master cylinders can seize.
• The clutch may seize if the plate becomes stuck to the flywheel because of corrosion.
• Handbrakes (parking brakes) can seize if the cables and linkages rust.
• Pistons can seize in the bores due to corrosion.

Fluids
• Old, acidic oil can corrode bearings.
• Uninhibited coolant can

Brake fluid should be renewed if any high-performance car has been sitting idle for months.

corrode internal waterways. Lack of antifreeze can cause core plugs to be pushed out, even cracks in the block or head. Silt settling and solidifying can cause overheating.
• Brake fluid absorbs water from the atmosphere and should be renewed every two years. Old fluid with a high water content can cause corrosion and pistons/callipers to seize (freeze) and can cause brake failure when the water turns to vapour near hot braking components.
• Even old petrol can deteriorate, resulting in poor running or failure to start.

Tyre problems

Tyres that have had the weight of the car on them in a single position for some time will develop flat spots, resulting in some (usually temporary) vibration. The tyre walls may have cracks or (blister-type) bulges, meaning new tyres are needed – problems

may be difficult to spot on ultra-low-profile sidewalls. It would be unwise to drive a high-performance machine like a Cosworth on its original rubber ...

Shock absorbers (dampers)

With lack of use, the dampers will lose elasticity or even seize. Creaking, groaning and stiff suspension are signs of this problem – although some modified Cosworths ride rather harshly and noisily anyway!

Rubber and plastic

Radiator hoses may have perished and split, possibly resulting in the loss of all coolant. Window and door seals can

Decidedly past its best – don't just add air and drive at 150mph!

harden and leak. Gaiters/boots can crack. Wiper blades will harden.

Electrics

• The battery will be of little use if it has not been charged for many months. Most Cosworths have aftermarket anti-theft alarm systems and immobilisers, which may drain power over a few days when not connected to a battery conditioner.
• Earthing/grounding problems are common when the connections have corroded. Old bullet- and spade-type electrical connectors commonly rust/corrode and will need disconnecting, cleaning and protection (eg Vaseline).
• Sparkplug electrodes will often have corroded in an unused engine.
• Wiring insulation can harden and fail.

Rotting exhaust system

Exhaust gas contains a high water content, so exhaust systems corrode very quickly from the inside when the car is not used. Most Cosworths wear aftermarket stainless systems, but they're not immune to rot.

16 The Community
– key people, organisations and companies in the Cosworth world

Thanks to its iconic status, Ford's RS Cosworth instantly gained a huge following among owners, clubs and marque specialists.

Today, there's no shortage of experts who will sell you a car, advise you on which to buy, tackle your servicing, supply you with spare parts, undertake a complete rebuild, or transform your Cossie into a fire-breathing track monster.

Many of these specialists have been dealing with Cosworths for decades, boasting the skills and experience to cope with any kind of problem or modification. That's why it's worth travelling to visit an expert rather than relying on local suppliers – especially for engine tuning and remapping.

Similarly, sourcing Cosworth parts can be fraught with problems, but most specialists have access to exactly the right components and accessories, often via mail order if you prefer to fit them yourself.

Clubs, websites and forums are equally useful for finding secondhand spares, along with advice and friendly banter (well, usually friendly!). Sign up if you're even thinking of buying a Cosworth – you'll gain invaluable information, and may discover your ideal car for sale online.

What's more, club registers retain important details about rare models; when investing in an RS500 in particular, consulting a club is an essential way to ensure it's completely legit.

Finally, if you're joining the Cosworth fraternity, indulging in fast Ford activities is part of the fun. From shows, track days and holiday tours to merchandise, magazines, spare parts and insurance deals, forum or club membership is a must.

Cosworths collected together at Ford Fair, one of Europe's leading events for blue oval enthusiasts.

Clubs and forums
Ford RS Owners' Club
www.rsownersclub.co.uk

Ford Sierra Owners' Club
www.fordsierraclub.co.uk

Ford RS Owners' Club of Australia
www.rsownersclubaust.com.au

Ford RS Owners' Club Ireland
www.rsownersclubireland.ie

Escort RS Cosworth Forum
www.escortrscosworth.com

PassionFord
www.passionford.com

RS500 owners' forum
www.rs500owners.com

Turbosport
www.turbosport.co.uk

RS Motorsport forum (Australia)
www.rsmotorsport.com.au

Specialists, parts and modifications
North Yorkshire RS Spares
01944 710368
www.cosworthrsspares.co.uk

Auto Specialists/Airtec
01375 850062
www.autospecialists.co.uk

Burton Power
020 8518 9136
www.burtonpower.com

Collins Performance
01260 279604
www.collinsperformance.com

CR Turbos
01425 638426
www.crturbos.co.uk

East Coast Classics
01944 710368
www.eccbikes.com

Field Motorsport
01245 320730
www.fieldmotorsport.com

Graham Goode Racing
0116 244 0080
www.grahamgoode.com

Grove Garage
01708 726518
www.grovegarage.com

Julian Godfrey Engineering
01435 865999
www.racetuners.com

MA Developments
07768 356204
www.madevelopments.com

Matt Lewis Motorsport
01922 692424
www.mattlewismotorsport.co.uk

Motorsport Developments
01253 508400
www.motorsport-developments.co.uk

Mountune
01277 226666
www.mountune.com

Norris Motorsport
01773 836274
www.norrismotorsport.co.uk

PJ Motorsport
01902 862882
www.pjmotorsportltd.co.uk

Rally Design
01227 792792
www.rallydesign.co.uk

SCS
01733 576614
www.specialistcarservices.com

Useful sources of information
***Classic Ford* magazine**
World-leading monthly magazine for classic Fords.

***Fast Ford* magazine**
The finest magazine for fast Ford owners.

17 Vital statistics
– essential data at your fingertips

Engine
Type: Ford Cosworth YBB/YBD/YBJ/YBG/YBP/YBT
Capacity: 1993cc
Bore/stroke: 90.82mm x 76.95mm
Compression ratio: 8.0:1

	Max power	Max torque
RWD	204bhp@6000rpm	205lb/ft@4500rpm
RS500	224bhp@6000rpm	206lb/ft@4500rpm
4x4	220bhp@6000rpm	214lb/ft@3500rpm
	(6250rpm with cat)	
Escort big-turbo	227bhp@6250rpm	224lb/ft@3500rpm
Escort small-turbo	217bhp@5750rpm	217lb/ft@2500rpm

Cylinders: four, in line
Cylinder head: cast alloy
Cylinder block: cast iron
Valve gear: four valves per cylinder, twin overhead camshafts, toothed belt drive
Induction: Weber-Marelli multi-point fuel-injection and electronic management system (all Sierras and Escort big-turbo) or Ford EEC IV engine management (small-turbo), Garrett turbocharger with intercooler
Ignition: Marelli/Ford electronic

Transmission
Sierra and Sapphire RWD
Rear-wheel drive with viscous coupling limited-slip differential
Gearbox: Borg Warner T5 five-speed manual
Internal ratios: 1st, 2.95:1; 2nd, 1.94:1; 3rd, 1.34:1; 4th, 1:1; 5th, 0.80:1
Final drive: 3.64:1

Sapphire 4x4 and Escort
Four-wheel drive with viscous coupling front and limited-slip viscous coupling rear differentials, 34/66 per cent front/rear split
Gearbox: MT75 five-speed manual
Internal ratios: 1st, 3.61:1; 2nd, 2.08:1; 3rd, 1.36:1; 4th, 1:1; 5th, 0.83:1
Final drive: 3.62:1

Suspension
Front: MacPherson struts, gas-filled dampers, coil springs, lower track control arms, 28mm anti-roll bar
Rear: independent, semi-trailing arms, coil springs, gas-filled dampers, 14mm anti-roll bar (Sierra three-door), 16mm anti-roll bar (Sapphire RWD), 18mm anti-roll bar (Sapphire 4x4), 22mm anti-roll bar (Escort)

Brakes
System: dual-circuit hydraulic with Teves ABS and vacuum servo assistance

	Front	Rear
RWD	283mm vented discs	273mm solid discs
4x4	278mm vented discs	273mm vented discs

Steering
Type: power-assisted rack and pinion, variable rate

Wheels and tyres
Sierra and Sapphire RWD: 7x15in RS alloys and 205/50 VR15 tyres
Sapphire 4x4: 7x15in RS alloys and 205/50 ZR15 tyres
Escort: 8x16in RS alloys and 225/45 ZR16 tyres

Dimensions

	Length	Width	Height
Sierra	175.5in (4458mm)	68in (1727mm)	54.2in (1377mm)
Sapphire	176.9in (4493mm)	66.8in (1697mm)	54.2in (1377mm)
Escort	165.8in (4211mm)	68.3in (1734mm)	56.1in (1425mm)

	Weight
Sierra	2651lb (1205kg)
RS500	2734lb (1240kg)
Sapphire RWD	2750lb (1250kg)
Sapphire 4x4	2822lb (1280kg)
Escort	2651lb (1275kg)

Performance figures

	Max speed	0-60mph
Sierra	149mph	6.2 seconds
Sapphire RWD	150mph	6.1 seconds
Sapphire 4x4	150mph	6.6 seconds
Escort big-turbo	140mph	5.9 seconds
Escort small-turbo	140mph	5.7 seconds

Production figures

	Total produced
Three-door	5542
RS500	500
Sapphire RWD	13,140
Sapphire 4x4	12,250
Escort	7145

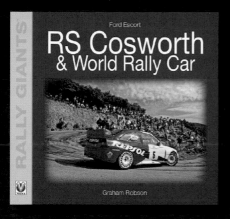

The Essential Buyer's Guide™ series ...